Life Cycle Risks
and the Politics of the
Welfare State

Carsten Jensen

Life Cycle Risks and the Politics of the Welfare State

Aarhus University Press

Life Cycle Risks and the Politics of the Welfare State
© Carsten Jensen and Aarhus University Press 2019
Cover, layout and typesetting: Nethe Ellinge Nielsen, Trefold
Publishing editor: Karina Bell Ottosen
This book is typeset in Sentinel and printed on 120 g Munken Lynx
Printed by Narayana Press, Denmark

Printed in Denmark 2019
ISBN 978 87 7184 982 0

Aarhus University Press
Finlandsgade 29
DK–8200 Aarhus N
Denmark
www.unipress.dk

Published with the financial support of Aarhus University Research Foundation

The Learned Society of Aarhus has recommended this book as the Acta Jutlandica
publication of the year

International distributors:
Oxbow Books Ltd.
The Old Music Hall
106–108 Cowley Road
Oxford, OX4 1JE
United Kingdom
www.oxbowbooks.com

ISD
70 Enterprise Drive, Suite 2
Bristol, CT 06010
USA
www.isdistribution.com

PEER
REVIEWED

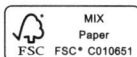

MIX
Paper
FSC FSC® C010651

This dissertation has been accepted by Aarhus BSS, Aarhus University,
for defence of the higher doctoral degree in Political Science.

Aarhus, 29 April 2019
Thomas Pallesen,
Dean

The defence will take place at 2.15 pm on 20 September 2019
at the Department of Political Science, Aarhus University, Denmark.

Contents

Foreword

This book is the summary report of my doctoral thesis. I would like to thank Christoffer Green-Pedersen, Henrik Bech Seeberg, Rune Slothuus, and David Weisstanner for reading an earlier version of the entire manuscript and for providing many useful suggestions for improvements. Troels Bøggild and Lasse Laustsen gave me valuable comments on Chapter 3. I also want to thank the committee —Christian Albrekt Larsen, Jonas Pontusson, and Svend-Erik Skaaning—for taking the time to comment thoroughly not only on this summary report, but on the book and articles that are part of the thesis as well. These stand-alone pieces are:

1. Carsten Jensen (2011). Marketization via compensation: health care and the politics of the right in advanced industrialized nations. *British Journal of Political Science, 41*(4), 907-926.
2. Carsten Jensen (2012). Labour market- versus life course-related social policies: understanding cross-programme differences. *Journal of European Public Policy, 19*(2), 275-291.
3. Carsten Jensen (2014). *The Right and the Welfare State.* New York and Oxford: Oxford University Press.

4. Christoph Arndt and Carsten Jensen (2017). Partivalg og holdninger til velfærdsstaten. In Kasper M. Hansen and Rune Stubager (eds.), *Oprør fra Udkanten: Folketingsvalget 2015.* Copenhagen: Djøf/Jurist- og Økonomforbundet, 245-263.
5. Carsten Jensen and Michael Bang Petersen (2017). The deservingness heuristic and the politics of health care. *American Journal of Political Science, 61*(1), 68-83.
6. Carsten Jensen, Christoph Arndt, Seonghui Lee, and Georg Wenzelburger (2018). Policy instruments and welfare state reform. *Journal of European Social Policy, 28*(2), 161-176.
7. Christoffer Green-Pedersen and Carsten Jensen (2019). Electoral Competition and the Welfare State. *West European Politics, 42*(4), 803-822.
8. Seonghui Lee, Carsten Jensen, Christoph Arndt, and Georg Wenzelburger (2019). Risky business? Welfare state reforms and government support in Britain and Denmark. *British Journal of Political Science.* Early view.

Karina Bell Ottosen and the people at Aarhus University Press have been very helpful with the publication of the book, which has been generously supported by a grant from Aarhus University Research Foundation.

Aarhus, July 2019

Chapter 1
Modernization, human biology, and a tale of two domains

The history of the welfare state begins with the industrial revolution. From the mid-19th century, Western societies began their momentous transformation from agricultural to industrial and, later, post-industrial economies. This process of modernization had two outcomes of particular interest to scholars of the welfare state. First, it commodified labor to an extent not seen before. Earning a wage income became essential for large segments of the populace. This, in turn, meant that losing one's job emerged as a serious risk. Without a job, poverty was a real threat for the new working class (Polyani 2001 [1944]; Wilensky and Lebeaux 1958). At the same time, commodification created the conditions for working-class mobilization and the subsequent political conflicts over society's material resources (Stephens 1979; Korpi 1983).

Second, modernization also created unprecedented wealth via rapid technological innovations and productivity growth. Over the course of the 20th century, Western societies became affluent, and part of their riches was spent to protect workers against the risks that modernization had created (Wilensky 1975). Workers became de-commodified, though to varying degrees depending on the strength and coalition opportunities of the parties and organizations advocating for their social rights. In some countries, de-commodification went a long way, and in others, less so. As time went by, these cross-national differences became institutionalized, effectively locking welfare states in on fairly rigid policy paths (Korpi 1989, 2006; Esping-Andersen 1990; Pierson 1994; van Kersbergen 1995; Huber and Stephens 2001; Iversen and Soskice 2009).

With the coming of the post-industrial economy, occupational structures changed and economies globalized, crafting new groups of (would-be) workers for whom the old welfare state institutions provided limited protection. Welfare state politics in the post-industrial era is about how best to deal with these new social risks. In the process, new coalitions have formed between social groups and their political representatives. The result has been a gradual transformation of job security regulation, unemployment benefit rules, and vocational training systems, as well as the expansion of leave policies and other rules meant to reconcile work and family life (Iversen and Wren 1998; Esping-Andersen 1999; Bonoli 2007; Emmenegger et al. 2012; Beramendi et al. 2015; Iversen and Soskice 2015).

In a nutshell, this is the politics of the welfare state as it has played itself out over the past more than one hundred years, or so the conventional wisdom would have it. The narrative overlooks one central fact. Modernization may have produced a set of labor market risks flowing from the commodification of the workforce in the 19th century; still, there exists a set of risks not created by modernization. These are risks caused by human biology and which threaten the physical integrity of an individual. These are *life cycle* risks.

Life cycle risks have a couple of features that make them categorically distinct from labor market risks. First, they existed long before modernization, although modernization has modified their concrete manifestation and the policies best suited to dealing with them. Second, while they may be risks people hope to avoid, they are at the same time part of almost everybody's expectation of a normal life: getting sick, getting old, dying. These life stages are simply part and parcel of the existence that most people want to live. They are, in a very fundamental way, facts of life. This is clearly not the case for labor market risks. Being unwillingly unemployed or underemployed is an anomaly to most people. Outside periods of massive downturns, being without work automatically means that you belong to a small minority. Contrary to the experience of life cycle risks, it is entirely possible to pass through one's time on Earth without being jobless or underemployed. Indeed, for most people, this is exactly what happens, give or take a few months after graduation or in between jobs.

In this thesis, I want to explore the politics of life cycle risks. My core claim is that because life cycle risks are a different type of risk from those of the labor market, the political dynamics surrounding them will be different too. The differences are apparent at all levels in the political process: from public preference formation over parties' efforts to maximize their vote share to public policy-making. Understanding the distinct political dynamics of life cycle and labor market risks, respectively, allows us to grasp several important empirical phenomena better: Why are some welfare programs much more—and much more universally—popular than others? Under what conditions will fiscal conservatives adopt a pro-welfare position? Why are some welfare programs characterized by a constant rise in public spending, while others have seen retrenchment?

These sorts of questions are vital for a research tradition that views the world through a very peculiar lens that, in some instances, disregards important variation and, in others, disregards equally important *in*variation. I argue that there is a big and politically salient variation between welfare programs aimed at life cycle and labor market risks, respectively. Health care and old age pensions are, for instance, systematically more popular and generously funded than unemployment protection and related labor market schemes, a difference that exists across the Western world. Most laypeople and scholars alike would, out of hand, agree with this observation, but we have no theoretical tools to understand why it exists.

Even more striking has been the neglect of invariation between countries regarding their management of life cycle risks. The welfare state literature is inherently comparative, meaning that it puts a heavy premium on cross-country variation. However, when it comes to life cycle risk protection, the similarities rather than the differences are what stand out. Extant research on old age pensions and health care is obsessed with institutional differences, of which there are many. Still, such institutional particularism has led to what Peter Baldwin aptly labels the narcissism of minor differences. What is amazing is not that affluent countries organize their life cycle risk protection in distinct ways, but that they all—without exception (and this includes the US)—prioritize this risk domain. From the perspective of human history, the mode of life cycle risk protection is much less important than the fact that there *is* life cycle risk protection.

Figure 1.1. The dual risk model of the welfare state

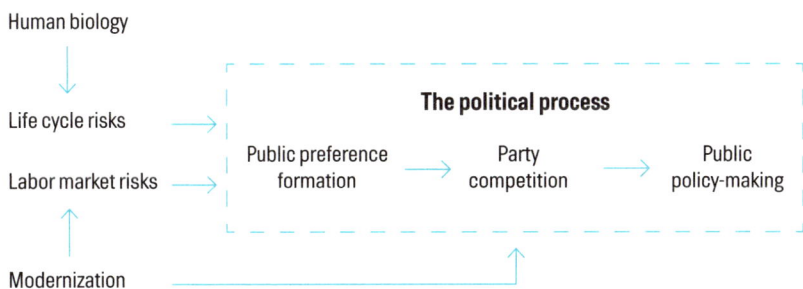

Figure 1.1 outlines the analytical framework of the thesis, which I call the *dual risk model of the welfare state*. In this stylized account, the political process is a product of the two primary sources of risks, namely human biology and modernization. Modernization is defined as the process of technological innovation and education of the workforce that, since the 19th century, has improved and to this day continues to improve both the physical and human capital of Western societies. As mentioned, modernization has two mostly unconnected effects. First is the creation of labor market risks—and with them working-class mobilization and class-based conflicts. Second is the secular rise in wealth and technological innovation. This latter effect plays equally important roles in the politics of life cycle and labor market risks, but in very diverse ways, as I will explain shortly.

In the dual risk model, the political process consists of a sequence of stages. The first stage is the preference formation of the public; the second stage sees parties compete for votes; and the third stage is public policy-making. In line with a huge body of research and in accordance with basic democratic ideals, I assume the political process to run "from the bottom up." This entails that public preferences causally affect party competition, which, in turn, affects public policy-making. Crucially, the previous stage does not *determine* the next. It is not possible to reduce public policies to the preferences of citizens or, for that matter, to the two underlying sources of risk. There are two reasons for this.

First, public preference formation is complex. Citizens normally have a fairly clear idea that they dislike exposure to social risks. Those exposed to risks want to be protected. However, the means by which such protection should be achieved is much less settled in the minds of most citizens. This leaves elite actors with considerable autonomy to pitch solutions that not only deliver protection, but also benefit special interests. The main obstacle to elite actors promoting a specific policy solution is that ordinary people exhibit substantial status quo bias. This means that they are inherently skeptical of new policies that radically change existing arrangements. Once a solution has been chosen, there is a bias against reform, which reform-oriented elite actors must consider when designing new policies (Pierson 1994).

Second, although public policies in an area as salient as the welfare state broadly reflect the public's preferences (Brooks and Manza 2007; Rehm 2011, 2016), concrete legislation is dependent on a host of bottlenecks and outside influences that can leave significant imprints on the final result. In political systems that are very fragmented, such as the US or Switzerland, small groups can block change supported by a majority of the citizenry (Tsebelis 2002), and interest groups can lobby for policies benefitting themselves at the expense of ordinary citizens (Hacker and Pierson 2010). A bottom-up model like the one I propose here can never explain the details and timing of individual pieces of legislation, which are normally put together by elite actors away from public scrutiny. What it should be able to explain, however, is the overall direction of policies and the consequent architecture of the welfare state.

Modernization, as noted, continues to affect the politics of risk protection. For labor market risks, this is a well-described phenomenon. The post-industrial economy has reshuffled the occupational structure of national economies, forced them open to global competition, and created new groups of insiders and outsiders (e.g., Esping-Andersen 1999; Häusermann 2010; Emmenegger et al. 2012; Thelen 2014; Beramendi et al. 2015; Iversen and Soskice 2015). Modernization also matters for life cycle risks. However, while modernization has altered the very nature of labor market risks themselves, when it comes to life cycle risks its main influence has been over the appropriate solutions. How are sickness and disability best treated? How do we ensure a dignified old age and a painless death? The answers to these questions are (luckily) not the same today as they were a hundred years ago. Technological innovation and higher living standards have vastly increased the expectations of citizens.

Importantly, these increasing expectations have caused a surging demand for life cycle risk protection, which, in turn, has forced governments to prioritize the scarce resources of the public purse. Life cycle risk protection, as a result, slowly crowds out the less popular labor market risk protection. The consequence is mounting inequality as the programs dedicated to the labor market outsiders are being cut, while the less redistributive life cycle risk programs enjoyed by everybody are being expanded. As such, the analysis of the politics of life cycle risks allows us to understand better the recent trend toward rising economic inequality in advanced democracies.

The purpose of this thesis is to explain and justify the dual risk model in Figure 1. Overall, the analytical framework should be viewed as a set of propositions—or, in the terminology of Popper (2002 [1963]: 43-86), bold conjectures—about how the politics of the welfare state play out. It is not within the scope of the thesis to test all the implied propositions, but I intend to deliver enough empirical evidence to be able to claim that the framework ought to be taken seriously. Here, I simply list the eight most prominent ones, noting that each of them contains multiple assumptions, or, if you will, supporting propositions, that I try to spell out further below. Essentially, these eight propositions also summarize my argument.

Proposition 1:
Individuals perceive the costs suffered from life cycle risks to be worse than the costs suffered from labor market risks.

Proposition 2:
Individuals perceive other individuals suffering from realized life cycle risks as more deserving than those suffering from realized labor market risks.

Proposition 3:
Cost and deservingness perceptions are much less amenable to elite framing in the domain of life cycle risks than in the domain of labor market risks.

Proposition 4:
Public support for government intervention is higher and more bipartisan in the domain of life cycle risks than in the domain of labor market risks.

Proposition 5:
All mainstream parties pay an equal amount of attention to life cycle risks, whereas there is a partisan bias in levels of attention in the domain of labor market risk.

Proposition 6:
Life cycle risk protection is prioritized over labor market risk protection in the policy-making process, leading to more generous protection overall.

Proposition 7:
In the domain of life cycle risk protection, partisan differences emerge only on second-order issues such as the institutional design of provision.

Proposition 8:
Over time, the prioritization of life cycle risk protection crowds out labor market risk protection, leading to rising exposure of labor market outsiders and increased economic inequalities.

The next chapter begins by establishing what I call the labor market bias of the existing literature, that is, the tendency of political scientists and historical sociologists to base most theorizing about welfare state development on the modernization process. As I argue, it is possible to distill something of a standard account of the welfare state. There is much to be appreciated in this standard account, and I am largely in agreement with it. However, unsurprisingly, it is most valuable when it comes to the risk domain it explicitly deals with, namely labor market risks. It has little to say about life cycle risks.

The subsequent chapter defines life cycle risks in some detail and contrasts the two risk types. It introduces some well-established ideas from psychology, which nevertheless are new to the welfare state literature. I thus aim to highlight just how fundamentally different the two risk domains are from each other. Chapter 4 outlines the core of the argument about the politics of life cycle risks and how this compares with the traditional politics of labor market risks. I emphasize that mine is a *dual* risk model, meaning that I fully recognize the importance of labor market risks and, by implication, the insights of the standard account of the welfare state—but that the other side of the coin, concerning life cycle risks, is equally important. The final chapter collects my thoughts on the rise in economic inequality and the future of the welfare state in light of the argument presented in the preceding chapters.

Table 1.1. The political process and the eight stand-alone pieces

	Public preference formation	Party competition	Public policy-making
The deservingness heuristic	X		
Risky business	X		
Partivalg og holdninger til velfærdsstaten	X		
Electoral competition and the welfare state		X	
Labor market versus life-course risks			X
Marketization via compensation			X
The Right and the welfare state	X	X	X
Policy instruments			X

The following four chapters should be read in conjunction with the seven papers and one book that are part of the thesis. These eight stand-alone pieces zoom in on various aspects of the political process as outlined in the analytical framework, but all ask the same basic question: What is the politics of risk protection? Throughout the current volume, I draw liberally on the arguments and empirical results presented in these previously published pieces to develop a single and coherent perspective on the politics of the welfare state that appreciates the role of both labor market and life cycle risks. To guide the reader, Table 1.1 summarizes how the book and papers relate to the three stages of the political process outlined in Figure 1.1.

Chapter 2
The labor market bias of the welfare state literature

This chapter looks at what I call the welfare state literature's labor market bias. This bias stems from the fact that the literature almost uniformly views the welfare state as a product of the modernization process that began in the 19th century and which continues to this day. The modernization process—understood as the technological innovations and education of the workforce that constantly upgrade society's physical and human capital—created the modern capitalist labor markets and thus formed the basis for the democratic class struggle over societies' material resources. In the wake of the post-industrial economy, the manifestation of this struggle has changed drastically, but modernization remains the underlying driver.

This chapter reviews the best-known and most influential pieces of work in the literature to document the labor market bias. I do not claim, of course, to make an exhaustive review. In fact, I am quite selective; I focus only on those books and articles that have presented elaborate theoretical accounts of the welfare state's development, deliberately skirting around the hundreds of pieces that are mainly empirical in scope. I do this because it is not important to my argument which of the various schools of thought are empirically correct (though, as I will try to show below, they are not as far removed from each other as is normally assumed); my aim is rather to establish their common theoretical blind spot. By zooming in on the research that has delivered the theoretical guidelines for the rest of the welfare state literature, this is what I hope to achieve.

Modernization and the origins of the welfare state literature

It is difficult within most fields of research to pinpoint the book or article that constitutes the start of it all. This is certainly true for the welfare state literature. Historical accounts of individual nations date back to the 19th century. Typically, they were written by historians or public intellectuals who wanted to describe the past or proscribe the future—or both, as was the case with, for instance, books by the Webbs in Britain or Steincke in Denmark. These early works do not offer synthetic arguments about the underlying political and economic causes of the welfare state. Rather, they present dense information about individual policies in individual countries in a given, limited period. Which aspects of these accounts are purely idiosyncratic and which aspects might potentially be relevant in a broader set of situations are unclear. For scholars wanting to learn how societies evolve, there is little to be gleaned from these early books—apart, of course, from the thick description—because they lack a theory of social development.

In this sense, Polyani's *The Great Transformation* (2001 [1944]) and Wilensky and Lebeaux's *Industrial Society and Social Welfare* (1958) are much better, and may arguably be viewed as the starting point of the welfare state literature. Although widely different in style and empirical analysis, they have much in common. First of all, they both outline a theory of how industrialization created a new type of risk that has fundamentally changed the human condition. Polyani's *The Great Transformation* is one of the undisputed masterpieces of social science. It explains how the rise of industrial capitalism implied a "fictitious commodification" of workers' labor power, where workers' labor is turned into a commodity to be sold and bought on the labor market like any other commodity. The only value of human capital is what it can fetch from an employer: the wage.

In a fully commodified labor market, wages are solely a function of the supply of labor from the workers and the demand for labor from the employers. Conversely, if workers have access to alternative income sources, the labor market will not clear because the supply of labor will be depressed. To emerge from the old agricultural economic order, industrial capitalism consequently required the systematic exposure of the workers to the risk of unemployment. This risk had to be manufactured by destroying workers' ability to make a living without a job (as happened via the enclosure movement that robbed smallholders of farmland), breaking up traditional community networks (which occurred when rural populations moved to the growing cities), and restricting access to poor relief (in the 1834 New Poor Law). The threat of unemployment became the gasoline that fueled industrialization.

Wilensky and Lebeaux's *Industrial Society and Social Welfare* is less well known than *The Great Transformation* outside the welfare state research community, but is a true classic within. The book mirrors Polyani's by investigating the effect of industrialization on the social organization of society, but this time focusing on the United States. The first insight from *Industrial Society and Social Welfare* is that industrialization created a set of novel risks in the United States too. In the words of the authors (Wilensky and Lebeaux 1958: 58),

> *In industry he [the worker] had nothing to sell but his labor and the employer bought it by the hour or the day. Should the workings of an impersonal market cast him in the role of unemployed, he had to hunt out another job [...] In short, the risks of an agricultural existence (even on a narrow margin above starvation) were spread widely among the extended family or whole village [...] The risk of an industrial existence were his; they were not so easily shared.*

24

However, there is more to the analyses of Polyani and Wilensky and Lebeaux than documenting the rise of the risk of unemployment. Both books also explore how the new risk created a demand for social protection (or "de-commodification" in the terminology of Esping-Andersen in *The Three Worlds of Welfare Capitalism*), which did not go unheard in either country. Polyani (2001 [1944]: 138-139), for instance, writes of the two opposing principles of economic liberalism and social protection, where the former led to the eventual prominence of the latter,

> *The one was the principle of economic liberalism, aiming at the establishment of a self-regulating market, relying on the support of the trading classes, and using largely laissez-faire and free trade as its methods; the other was the principle of social protection aiming at the conservation of man and nature as well as productive organization, relying on the varying support of those most immediately affected by the deleterious action of market—primarily, but not exclusively, the working and the landed classes—and using protective legislation, restrictive associations, and other instruments of intervention as its methods.*

This connection between labor market risks and demand for social protection is analytically crucial. It has influenced almost all branches of the welfare state literature because it creates a plausible link between the realm of socio-economics and the realm of politics, and thereby suggests *why* the welfare state came about. Moreover, this "logic of industrialism" has a claim to universality because the process of industrialization shares core characteristics everywhere; most importantly, of course, the risk of unemployment.

In the 1960s and 1970s, several authors tested this proposition. In *Welfare Policy and Industrialization in Europe, America and Russia* (1971), Rimlinger explores the origins of the welfare state by employing in-depth historical case studies. He shows that while national trajectories varied due to socio-political contexts, industrialization was a core driver everywhere as it created both new demands and new opportunities for provision of social protection. Using quantitative data from countries around the globe, Cutright (1965) and Wilensky (1975) present analyses that supplement the in-depth case studies of Rimlinger. In an influential article covering 76 countries, Cutright (1965) shows that various proxies of modernization such as energy consumption, urbanization, and literacy are strongly correlated with the number of years for which, by 1960, a given country had had experience of five different welfare programs. In *The Welfare State and Equality*, Wilensky expands on the conclusion of Cutright. Using per capita GDP as a proxy of modernization across 60 countries, Wilensky shows how more affluent countries are very often also equipped with more generous welfare states, measured as the proportion of GDP allocated to income maintenance.

Taken together, these conclusions prove that industrialization was pivotal in the emergence of the welfare state. It led to the breakdown of the traditional forms of social protection and effectively created mass unemployment as a new form of risk concerning the wellbeing of workers. To most workers, this first step in the modernization process meant a severe increase in exposure to financial ruin for themselves and their nearest family. However, industrialization also created the means to protect themselves against the new risk. As countries became richer, they gradually expanded the welfare state. In the mid-19th century, no country in the world had a welfare state, but a hundred years later all Western democracies had introduced extensive social protection. In the context of human history, this constitutes an extremely rapid change.

The outline here has become something of a conventional wisdom; so much so that the core works are rarely cited anymore. In their stead came a new generation of research that focused on cross-country variation within affluent Western democracies. Whereas the logic of industrialism had been preoccupied with understanding the universal or ultimate cause of the welfare state—why all affluent countries developed a welfare state in the first place—the research that emerged from the late 1970s onward cared about the big differences in the way welfare states are organized. Although very different in the ways they account for these differences, they virtually all share the same underlying assumption, namely that the welfare state, at its heart, is a product of the modernization process.

Power resources and political conflict

The power resource theory holds that the welfare state differs across countries because the power resources of those wanting to promote generous welfare state arrangements—above all else the labor movement—vary. Stephens's *The Transition from Capitalism to Socialism* (1979) and Korpi's *The Democratic Class Struggle* (1983) are two of the foundational pieces in the tradition. Both emphasize the critical role of industrial capitalism in the emergence of the welfare state. In the words of Stephens (1979: 39-40—where the term "socialism" de facto means "the welfare state," cf. p. 72),

> *Capitalism has created the material basis for socialism in the advanced capitalist democracies. Concentration, the accumulation of capital, has created sufficient affluence that socialization would not mean just generalization of poverty. Centralisation has proceeded to the point where the entire Western economy is dominated by huge oligopolistic corporations [...] Aside from creating the material base for socialism, concentration and centralisation have an important indirect effect on the de-*

velopment of socialism. They promote labour organization.

The argument of Stephens and Korpi is, in a nutshell, that industrialization simultaneously created both the economic wealth needed to finance protection for the new working class and the collective actors willing to fight for the redistribution of wealth this necessarily entails. However, the strength of labor movements differed between countries and over time. Where either the industrial structure was fragmented, or ethno-religious cleavages cut across the economic cleavage, workers were less likely to mobilize into a strong and coherent labor movement that could fight for their material interests. These differences in labor movement mobilization to a large extent explain why some countries ended up with big and others with small welfare states.

The early works in the power resource tradition put particular emphasis on unions as the core promoters of workers' interests. Although acknowledging the role of parties, the parliamentary arena is largely viewed as the transmission belt connecting the labor market with policies. Esping-Andersen's *Politics against Markets* (1985) provides a corrective to this focus, though the book remains firmly within the boundaries of the power resource theory. Esping-Andersen observes that working-class parties, above all else the social democrats, rarely had a parliamentary majority alone. As such, they were dependent on forming alliances with other social groups to promote their policy preferences. When alliances were off the table, the pro-welfare forces in society were too weak to have much of an impact. On the other hand, the reason Scandinavia developed such generous welfare states comes down to the alliance between the social democrats and (small-holding) farmers (Esping-Andersen 1985: 72-73):

> *For social democracy, the most decisive characteristic of the Scandinavian countries has been the farmers' capacity for self-organization, which set the stage for an internationally unique alliance between liberal farmers and socialist workers. The independent, and politically quite powerful, position of the farmers also meant a more disunited bourgeois bloc. In contrast, the social democrats, backed by the powerful trade union movement, have usually had little to fear from the left.*

The insight that generous welfare states are dependent on coalitions of different socio-economic groups has had a lasting influence on the literature. Iversen and Soskice (2006), for instance, formalize the argument and stress the importance of electoral institutions in the probability of center-left coalitions forming, yet the book's greatest influence has been on the study of Christian democracy in continental Europe. Stephens (1979: 40-46) and Korpi (1983: 26-45), as noted, had already pointed to the fact that the traditional labor movements tend to be weaker in countries with cross-cutting cleavages, which, in the context of continental Europe, especially means that between Catholics and Protestants. Esping-Andersen's *Three Worlds of Welfare Capitalism* (1990) nuances this observation by showing that this does not imply that continental European welfare states are necessarily less generous overall than Scandinavian ones, but only that the redistributive profile is very different. In continental European welfare states, a prime objective is status maintenance, meaning that the welfare state is designed to uphold existing class distinctions. In Scandinavia, in contrast, welfare benefits tend to be the same for all claimants, disregarding their former work history.

In *Social Capitalism* (1995), van Kersbergen explores the political causes behind this outcome. He shows how Christian democratic parties emerged after World War II with the aim of embracing not least Catholic churchgoers from both the working and middle classes. Rather than cross-class coalitions of parties, as in Scandinavia, continental Europe saw cross-class coalitions within a single party, namely the Christian Democrats. This led to the peculiar policy mix that still characterizes this part of Europe. The traditionalists in the Catholic Church and the Christian democratic parties preferred the traditional family structure with a single earner, a male breadwinner. The workers, as everywhere else, wanted protection against labor markets risks. The solution that made the cross-class coalition acceptable to both sides was elaborate protection for the male breadwinner in the form of hefty employment protection and generous income maintenance schemes that reflected one's work history, but much less generous protection for everybody else. This offered protection to most of the workers at the time, but in a way that clearly favored traditional male breadwinner households.

Stephens (1979), Korpi (1983), Esping-Andersen (1985), and van Kersbergen (1995) are all firmly rooted in the power resource theory. As such, they all focus on classes and class conflict. Stephens (1979) and Korpi (1983) have a rather simple understanding of how this conflict plays itself out, arguing that the stronger the unions of the labor movements are, the bigger the welfare state will be. Esping-Andersen (1985) and van Kersbergen (1995) highlight the importance of party politics, yet the underlying conclusion is the same for all four authors: Welfare states are a function of how much power individual classes can aggregate and how successfully they can bring it to bear in the parliamentary arena.

Business interests and corporatist bargains

The power resource theory is, at its heart, an argument about social conflict between the haves and the have-nots. Other theories view the development of the welfare state in more consensual terms, arguing that business may not always be as opposed to the welfare state as the power resource theory assumes.

Katzenstein's *Small States in World Markets* from 1985 is the paradigmatic example of such an approach. Katzenstein asks how the small nations of Europe, with their powerful labor movements, have been able to respond effectively to the demands of globalization. Small open economies must compete in world markets that require them to keep prices low and the production system flexible to meet shifting demands. To keep prices low, wages must be kept relatively low too, and flexibility essentially entails less employment security and on-the-job rights for workers. None of this ought to be acceptable to those representing the workers' interests. Strangely, however, it is in the countries of the world where the labor movement has been strongest that wage moderation and labor market flexibility have been most pronounced. The answer to the puzzle is, according to Katzenstein (1985: 24), that

> *Elites in small European states, while letting international markets force economic adjustments, choose a variety of economic and social policies that prevent the costs of change from causing political eruptions. They live with change by compensating for it.*

The compensation comes in a variety of forms, but the welfare state takes pride of place. When workers must live with the risk of joblessness, they must be protected against potential income loss via generous unemployment protection programs. With comparably low wages, access to otherwise costly services such as education and health care must be provided by the government.

A crucial point in Katzenstein's analysis is that the labor movement did not invent the competitiveness-for-compensation nexus. Rather, it is a product of decades' worth of corporatist negotiations among business interests, the labor movement, and the government. It is these corporatist arrangements that Katzenstein singles out as the main cause of the emergence of big welfare states in Scandinavia and other small European countries such as the Netherlands and Austria.[1] In this formulation (Katzenstein 1985: 32):

> *Corporatism is distinguished by three traits: an ideology of social partnership expressed at the national level; a relatively centralized system of interest groups; and a voluntary and informal coordination of conflicting objectives through continuous political bargaining between interest groups, state bureaucracies, and political parties. These traits make for a low-voltage politics.*

---

1   'Corporatism' used to have several meanings and can refer to non-democratic regimes such as Italy under Mussolini. Katzenstein, therefore, labelled his form of corporatism "democratic corporatism." Today, these older connotations are no longer remembered, so I simply refer to 'corporatism'.

Katzenstein tracks the origins of corporatism back to the 1930s and 1940s, when a series of highly antagonistic confrontations between the labor movement and business ended with compromises that settled certain rules of the game for future interactions between business and labor. Over time, the actors involved learned to see the economic advantage of the new situation, and what Katzenstein calls an ideology of social partnership slowly emerged. It became the norm to negotiate and to search out compromises that everybody could accept, if not necessarily love. For the labor movement, a competitive economy helped secure full employment and the associated compensation was of great value to the workers; all in all, a fair price to be paid for modest employment protection and workplace rights. For business, accepting higher taxes to finance the welfare state was a reasonable price to pay for the ability to compete in the world market.

Katzenstein's account of the emergence of the welfare state puts more emphasis on bipartisan consensus than the power resource theory does, but it is also clear that the differences are not overwhelming. In Katzenstein's account, business and labor were historically pitched against each other, and even under a system of corporatism, actors' interests will not converge perfectly. It is therefore only natural that Garrett, in *Partisan Politics and the Global Economy* (1998), makes an explicit attempt at combining the two perspectives. Garrett argues that large welfare states require both entrenched corporatism arrangements and a strong left-wing presence in parliament. Without corporatism, strong left-wing parties will introduce policies detrimental for economic performance, and without strong left-wing parties, the corporatist actors will not face enough impetus to make the radical decisions needed to reach the competitiveness-for-compensation nexus.

While Garrett tries to pull the corporatism and power resource theories together, the academic debate of the early 2000s saw some attempts at pulling them apart. Swenson, in his aptly titled *Capitalist against Markets* (2002), shows how American and Swedish welfare state legislation in the 1930s, 1940s, and early 1950s often happened with the consent and, sometimes, outright support of businesses. As Swenson (2002: 12) puts it,

> *Capitalists often like government regulation when they see a net benefit and little risk. Like a powerful solvent, interests often quickly dissolve ideological sentiments against advantageous government regulation. Welfare policies can provide just such intervention. To say that capitalists have interests in reform is not, however, to say that they always act according to those interests as opposed to competing ones, institutional constraints, free-market liberalism, or just plain stick-in-the-mudism.*

Business has, in other words, from time to time played a much more independent and proactive role in the formation of the welfare state than the power resource theory assumes. Rather than being universally opposed to welfare programs, the interests of business varied greatly between Sweden and the US and over time, depending on the system of wage-setting (what Swenson calls "segmentalism") and price-setting ("cartelism"). Adding to Swenson's approach, Mares outlines an encompassing theory of the welfare-friendly role of business in her *The Politics of Social Risks* (2003). Mares argues that whether business will support the welfare state and, more exactly, what kind of welfare state it will support, depends on the composition of firms in the country. In so-called high-risk industries, large firms with high skills intensity production will, for instance, support more contributory insurance arrangements, while small firms with low skills intensity will favor more universalistic policies. In low-risk industries, the same small firms with low skills intensity will oppose the welfare state outright.

Both Swenson's and Mares's accounts highlight how business may not always be the welfare-hating antagonist that the power resource theory appears to suggest. Both books are, moreover, quite nuanced. Nowhere is there a claim that business always welcomed, let alone pushed for, big welfare states—and when it did take on a proactive role, it was strictly to maximize the profit of the firm. As Mares (2003: 23) writes, "The costs of social policy for employers do not always outweigh the benefits provided by social policy to firms." It is also worth noting that Swenson's and Mares's empirical analyses mainly concern periods (from the late 19th century until right after World War II) and places (Germany, France, and the USA, though also Sweden) where the labor movement was comparably weak. This is important because it hints that the business-centered approach and the power resource theory may be supplementary. The power resource theory is, according to its own founding fathers, about the expansion of welfare states in the golden age from the 1950s to the 1970s. Conversely, for those times and places without a labor movement of import, other explanations are obviously needed for why some modicum of social protection did in fact come about.[2]

2 I do not wish to push this point too far since Korpi (2006) engaged in a highly critical review of Swenson (2002) and Mares (2003). That critique has, itself, been the subject of discussion (see, e.g., Iversen and Soskice 2009; Swenson 2017). Still, in my view, the differences between the power resource theory and historically sensitive business-centered case studies have been overblown. One reason for this is the academic fashion for studying "origins": the origins of welfare states, the origins of electoral systems, the origins of federalism, the origins of business associations, etc. From the perspective of the welfare state, this means that some scholars become highly invested in specific starting dates. Business-centered scholars tend to argue that the welfare state emerged around the turn of the 19th century (when the labor movement could not have mattered much), while power resource theorists argue that this happened only from the 1930s and, especially, after World War II (the heyday of the labor movement). For dispassionate observers, both arguments have merit. Some of the core institutions were, indeed, settled before the labor movement became a force to be reckoned with, but it is also true that the vast bulk of expansion happened only in the middle part of the 20th century.

Later work within the business-centered approach has arguably vulgarized the original insights of Swenson (2002) and Mares (2003) by switching from historical case studies of concrete reform instances within individual countries to a much more aggregated perspective, where clusters of countries are compared using data covering the past few decades. In this line of analysis, known as the varieties of capitalism approach, all employers in the so-called coordinated market economies (basically all of Western Europe except Britain and Ireland) are supposed to be relatively pro-welfare, while all employers in liberal market economies (all Anglo-Saxon countries) are supposed to be opposed. However, one does not have to accept this sort of sweeping—and many country experts would probably say implausible—claim to appreciate that actors other than the workers and their representatives can promote welfare state development.

The rise of the post-industrial economy

All the theories reviewed so far are concerned with the emergence of the welfare state from the turn of the 19th century until the 1970s. By around 1980 the distinct welfare state regimes had crystalized into a universal Scandinavian model, a residual Anglo-Saxon model, and an insurance-based continental

European model.[3] Each model had its distinct institutional logic, which generated powerful feedback effects that, in political terms, made them self-maintaining (Esping-Andersen 1990). However, at the same time, the preconditions behind the welfare state began to change as industrialization gave way to post-industrialization and a transformed set of labor market risks. In the words of Esping-Andersen (1999: 5),

Contemporary welfare states and labour market regulations have their origins in, and mirror, a society that no longer obtains: an economy dominated by industrial production with strong demand for low-skilled workers; a relative homogenous and undifferentiated, predominantly male, labour force (the standard production worker); stable families with high fertility; and a female population primarily devoted to housewifery. Welfare regimes are built around a set of egalitarian ideals and risk profiles that predominated when our parents and grandparents were young.

3   There has been a lively debate about the exact numbers of regimes. Some argue that there exists a Southern European model (Ferrera 1996), and others that there is such a thing as a wage-earner model in Australia and New Zealand (Castles 1994). From my viewpoint, this is not so important since all the alternatives rest on a re-specification of well-known theoretical (labor market-oriented) factors. They are, in other words, situated squarely within the mainstream of the welfare state literature.

In the post-industrial economy, service employment has become the norm, female participation rates have soared, and many households no longer have a male breadwinner. All welfare states, and especially those in continental Europe, have been bad at handling these new developments, effectively leaving a large share of the population without proper income protection. It is only natural, therefore, that the research community has over the past couple of decades redirected much of its attention to the politics of the welfare state in this new post-industrial reality.

Iversen and Wren (1998) presented an early analysis of what they call the trilemma of the service economy, which has influenced much subsequent thinking. They argue that the rising number of service jobs forces governments to prioritize two out of three goals: fiscal discipline, earnings equality, and employment growth. A country has two of these desirable outcomes, but not all three, and it turns out that there is a systematic pattern in which countries opt for what outcomes. The Anglo-Saxon countries go for fiscal discipline and employment growth; the Scandinavian ones choose employment growth and earnings equality; and in continental Europe, fiscal discipline and earnings equality hold sway. This reinforces old patterns, with rising inequality in places such as Britain and the US, as well as swelling numbers of labor market outsiders in continental Europe.

The increasing prominence of the insider-outsider divide—where one part of the labor force enjoys extensive employment protection and another part is left either jobless or with low-paid and fixed-term "junk jobs"—may be the one aspect of the post-industrial economy that has received the most attention from scholars. Rueda's *Social Democracy Inside Out* (2007) is a good example. Rueda argues that social democratic parties have changed their policy position since the 1970s as a response to the increasing salience of the insider-outsider divide. The parties have shifted from being workers' parties to become parties for the insiders. Insiders are typically more unionized and more active voters than the outsiders, meaning that their interests are more likely to be heard and their frustrations more likely to matter electorally. In many European countries, the rational strategy for vote-maximizing social democrats has, therefore, been to heed the policy preferences of the insiders more than those of the outsiders. This essentially implies that existing insider biases have tended to strengthen when social democratic parties have ruled.

The insider-outsider divide not only affects the position of individual parties but also more broadly transforms how welfare state reforms are undertaken. In *The Politics of Welfare State Reform in Continental Europe* (2010), Häusermann shows how post-industrialization's fragmentation of the occupational structure has created a political landscape in which new and old classes enter into coalitions in sometimes surprising ways. The core insight of Häusermann is that the rise of outsiders has turned the old-fashioned welfare state politics into a multidimensional game where political exchange is made easier. For Häusermann, this helps explain why continental Europe has witnessed considerably more reform activity than might be expected given the entrenched position of the insiders. The insurance-based welfare state model has produced much opposition to change from those benefitting from the system, but, precisely because it has left so many as outsiders, reforms eventually did happen.

The notion that the post-industrial occupational structure has paved the way for new class coalitions has sparked much research in recent years. Thelen's *Varieties of Liberalization and the New Politics of Social Solidarity* (2014), for instance, introduces dynamic cross-class coalition-building into the varieties of capitalism approach to understand better contemporary labor market policies in Denmark, Germany, and the US. Following a similar line of inquiry, Iversen and Soskice (2015) show that countries differ in their response to economic shocks depending on the underlying class coalitions and the position of the labor market outsiders in them. Beramendi et al. (2015), finally, present what is arguably the most encompassing synthesis of the coalitional politics of post-industrial welfare states. The authors explain how the arrival of the new occupational structure has directed the realignment between different voter groups and parties, as well as how this has ultimately decided the relative priority given to consumption (passive unemployment benefits and various pension schemes) and investment (education and active labor market policies) in modern welfare states.

Another important line of research on the effects of post-industrialism has focused on gender. Early feminists such as Lewis (1992) and Orloff (1993) pointed out how existing welfare state research overlooked women by assuming that the big issues at stake were income protection against unemployment and, more broadly, decommodification. Given that many, if not most, females were not even commodified, it made no sense to talk about de-commodification. Over time, female participation rates have increased significantly, but gender equality is still a distant goal. Almost everywhere, females constitute the main group of outsiders. Women, much more frequently than men, have part-time and fixed-term jobs, and they are generally underpaid compared to their male colleagues. Several authors such as Häusermann (2010), Iversen and Rosenbluth (2010), and Morgan (2013) have explored how women-cum-employees feature in the new politics of post-industrial welfare states.

Taken together, the labor market bias of the literature on post-industrialism and the welfare state is evident. Just as earlier approaches took their analytical cue from industrialization to understand how unemployment became a major social risk and the democratic class struggle between workers and business played itself out, so post-industrialism is seen as the source of additional labor market risks and transformed political coalitions. Many modern-day workers must not only fear ending up without a job but will also have to live with an increasingly precarious employment situation of fixed-term contracts, reduced workplace rights, and an inability to reconcile work and family life. As a result, the political consequences of this reshuffling of the occupational structure have preoccupied the literature.

The sources of citizens' preferences

One of the recurrent debates in the welfare state literature is about which factors affect citizens' formation of social policy preferences. Two main factors have dominated the literature, namely redistribution of income from the well-off to the less well-off and insurance against future income loss. The logic of industrialism contained little explicit thinking about the sources of citizens' preferences, so it is only with the power resource theory that a concerted effort was made to sort out the micro-level foundations behind the macro-level arguments (although it took until the 2000s for stricter empirical tests to be used to discriminate between the various explanations).

To the power resource scholars, it is redistribution that drives people's preferences. As formulated by Korpi (1983: 83), the welfare state is meant to "compensate labor for its disadvantaged position in the labor market [...] by redistributing income between different groups of citizens." Esping-Andersen's famous concept of de-commodification entails the same sort of redistribution, since the purpose of de-commodification is to "emancipate workers from market dependence" and to "minimize the importance of market-generated income" (Esping-Andersen 1990: 26). In this line of reasoning, workers want a big welfare state because it (partly) nullifies existing discrepancies in labor market income. Likewise, business and the bourgeois oppose a big welfare state because it requires that they forego some of their income as taxes.

Melzer and Richards (1981) started another tradition in the welfare state literature by combining the median voter model of Downs with the notion of redistributive preferences. According to the Meltzer-Richards model, the fact that the median voter's income in countries with universal suffrage will always be lower than the mean income of society means that the median voter will stand to gain from downward redistribution—and since the median voter decides policy, redistribution will duly occur. The central macro-level prediction of the Melzer-Richards model—that countries with high market inequality will see more redistribution than countries with low market inequality—has received only limited empirical support. As such, the Meltzer-Richards model's influence lies in the fact that many political economy arguments have taken its basic assumptions as their starting points: The median voter earns less than the mean income in society and therefore wants redistribution.

In *The Politics of Social Solidarity,* Baldwin (1990) provides a different perspective on preferences. To him, people are primarily motivated not by redistribution of current levels of income but by insurance against losing it in the future. It is the risk of future income loss that really matters. Baldwin's core insight is thus that a society's risk groups do not necessarily overlap with its income groups. In particular, the poor may not always be those most exposed to a certain risk, allowing for a potential coalition that cuts across the income distribution and, hence, classic partisan divides. In Baldwin's (1990: 12, 18) formulation,

> *Although it may have suffered more than its share of risks, the proletariat has had no monopoly on uncertainty or on an interest in measures to ameliorate such circumstances [...] Because risk categories and classes are disjoint in this sense, coalitions of interest in a reapportioning of burdens have been negotiated that are far more complex and socially multifarious than the usual binary approach to disputes over social policy: proletariat against bourgeois, poor versus rich.*

Baldwin's work is often picked out as the first to employ an explicit risk perspective on the development of the welfare state, and my argument is inspired by the intuition behind his. However, while Baldwin's argument is innovative, it is important to realize that his conceptualization of risks is both broad and underspecified. It includes everything from the risks that ordinary citizens can suffer (ending up without an income and therefore needing unemployment protection or old age pensions) to the risks of collective actors (such as firms or farmers going out of business and therefore needing agricultural subsidies and preferential tax treatments). To Baldwin, any risk against the future income of a social group creates a potential for coalition formation.

This, naturally, makes for a highly flexible analytical framework, but also one that is impossible to falsify beyond the notion that a preference for insurance against income loss is what motivates actors. In fact, it is so broad that it is difficult to see why Baldwin's conceptualization of risk protection is not a subcategory of Esping-Andersen's (1990: 26) concept of de-commodification, which, as noted before, is defined as policies aimed to "minimize the importance of market-generated income." Baldwin, moreover, argues that his risk categories allow him to analyze cross-class coalition formation. However, by the time *The Politics of Social Solidarity* was published, the power resource theory he pitched his argument against had already moved away from "the binary approach" of Stephens (1979) and Korpi (1983) to the coalitional perspective of Esping-Andersen (1985). So, while the concept of insurance against risks is valuable, its analytical purchase in Baldwin's analysis is actually rather limited. The underlying reason for this is that Baldwin has a very contextual understanding of the relevant sources of risks against future income. That is, he never specifies a general argument about what causes risks that can be inferred beyond the five historical cases he studies. This allows him to describe the concrete historical trajectories but also makes the insights of his work difficult to generalize.[4]

However, much thinking has been dedicated to specifying what the source of risks might be, to allow for a more systematic analysis than Baldwin's, especially since the early 2000s. Iversen and Soskice (2001: 876) present the most famous specification. In their theory,

> *Workers derive their income from skills that can be either general or specific. Specific skills are valuable only to a single firm or a group of firms (whether an industry or a sector), whereas general skills are portable across all firms.*

This distinction between specific (non-portable) and general (portable) skills is important in the case of unemployment. An unemployed person with general skills will typically have a much easier time finding a new job precisely because his or her skills are valuable to a broad set of firms. An unemployed person with specific skills will, on the other hand, have a harder time finding a new job because his or her skills are much more tied to one or a few firms. Skills specificity, in sum, is a source of risk against

---

4   To be fair, Baldwin never claims that this is his aim—and as a historian, it is not obvious why he would want to make a generalizable political science theory.

future income. Unemployment protection and job security schemes are straightforward ways of insuring against the risk, so the ultimate expectation of Iversen and Soskice is that skills specificity is positively correlated with support for these sorts of welfare state programs. Using cross-national survey data from 16 countries in the mid-1990s, the authors present micro-level evidence that this is indeed the case. Interestingly, Iversen and Soskice's results also show that income is consistently negatively correlated with welfare state support. The richer a person is, the less likely he is to favor a big welfare state. This essentially corroborates the assumption of both the power resource theory and the Meltzer-Richards model, suggesting that citizens may want both insurance and redistribution at the same time.[5]

Moene and Wallerstein (2001) and Rehm (2011) are well-known advocates of such an integrated approach, in which citizens are assumed to care about maximizing their current level of labor market income as well as maximizing protection against future income loss. Moene and Wallerstein (2001: 490) present a formal model that squares the circle by assuming that "the demand for insurance rises as income increases" and that the risk of unem-

5   In their empirical analysis, Iversen and Soskice study support for social spending. Yet there is an argument to be made that the fairer test of the power resource theory and Meltzer-Richards model is to look at preference for redistribution directly. Many cross-national surveys contain a question that taps this (typically something like: "Do you agree or disagree that the government should take measures to reduce differences in income levels?"). Using this formulation, the correlation with income (as well as other measures of current wealth) becomes even stronger.

ployment is distributed identically across countries. However, as Rehm (2011) shows, neither of these assumptions are correct empirically. Better-off individuals demand less insurance than those with less income, even though they, in absolute terms, have more to lose, and the correlation between the risk of unemployment and income differs significantly from one country to the next.

Rehm's alternative explanation is ingenious and highly intuitively plausible. He starts by arguing that a person's preferences for unemployment protection are a dual function of income and risk of unemployment. Low income and high unemployment risk both predict support for generous unemployment protection. In the next step, Rehm proposes that countries vary regarding how much overlap there is between the income distribution and the risk of unemployment. In some countries the overlap is big; that is, the poor are also overwhelmingly the ones suffering from the risk of joblessness. In other countries the overlap is small, meaning that people higher up the income distribution also suffer from the risk of unemployment. Politically, this makes all the difference because it brings the median voter on board in the pro-welfare state coalition. The degree of overlap between income and risk of unemployment emerges as an important factor accounting for cross-national variation in the generosity of unemployment protection schemes.

By integrating the redistribution and risk perspectives at the micro-level, Rehm helped spark a burgeoning literature on welfare state preferences.

The main thrust of the literature is preoccupied with understanding more precisely which segments of the public are exposed to risks and under what circumstances this leads to more or less support for redistribution, unemployment protection, employment security, and so on (e.g., Gingrich and Ansell 2012; Wren and Rehm 2014; Häusermann et al. 2016; Alt and Iversen 2017). Taken together, this new micro-level focus has yielded much—and much-needed—insight into the underlying assumptions of the welfare state literature. The dichotomous discussion between those favoring the redistribution and insurance views, respectively, is basically finished. As in the case of the new work on post-industrial welfare state politics, this has allowed for a much more refined understanding of the social world.

Institutions

When I claim that the welfare state literature suffers from a labor market bias, I do so because all the major driving forces of the welfare state hark back to the modernization process. Industrialization created the risk of unemployment and the social classes that fought over the organization of society, while post-industrialization created a new, heterogeneous group of labor market outsiders and reshuffled the linkages between labor market groups and parties. I will even go so far as to claim that the labor market bias constitutes something of a paradigm, a common but implicit denominator of the major theoretical accounts on welfare state development.

This does not mean, however, that all work in the welfare state literature is directly concerned with the modernization process. Since the 1990s, scholars have explored how today's political decisions are structured by preexisting institutions.[6] Authors such as Pierson (1994), Streeck and Thelen (2005), and Palier (2010) have investigated how existing welfare state institutions tend to direct new policies, ensuring that most reforms will be incremental, though not necessarily inconsequential, in nature. From my perspective, the critical point about this approach is that institutions are almost always viewed as upholding or undermining the outcomes that the politics of the modernization process created. The reform trajectory of Germany is different from the reform trajectory of Sweden because the former has the welfare state that the "within-party" coalition of the Christian Democrats made, whereas the latter has the welfare state that the "between-party" coalition of the social democrats and small centrist parties produced. In my view, this is a fine example of the paradigmatic power of the labor market bias; even authors who are not explicitly working on the topic take it as their starting point.

6   Welfare state institutionalism is, in fact, closely connected to the post-industrialism literature reviewed above. As such, much of this literature also suffers from an explicit labor market bias on top of the implicit one I identify here.

Formal political institutions, notably veto points and electoral systems, have also received sustained attention and would appear to defy the labor market bias. Veto points are constitutionally guaranteed rights to block or slow legislation enjoyed by, for example, a second chamber, federal states, or the legal system (Immergut 1990; Tsebelis 2002). The presence of veto points has been used to explain why some countries' welfare states are smaller than one might expect given the strength of their labor movements, and why retrenchment-oriented politicians may be less successful than their nominal strength would suggest (Huber et al. 1993; Pierson 2001). There is little doubt that veto points can be important for concrete legislative processes, but only as a moderator of actors' ability to pursue their existing preferences. Veto points cannot and are not meant to explain why actors want what they do, only whether they can get it or not; preferences are exogenously given. In this critical sense, the veto point theory is not a theory of welfare state development because it has no notion of what motivates individuals.

While veto points affect the ability of parties to set policy, electoral systems affect the strength parties have in parliament in the first place and how likely they are to be in government. As mentioned previously, Iversen and Soskice (2006) argue that the electoral system biases government formation: proportional representation leading to more center-left governments and first-past-the-post systems leading to more center-right governments, an outcome which, in accordance with the power resource theory, leads to more redistribution. Manow and van Kersbergen (2009) expand this argument to include Christian democracy and the continental European experience, and the general insight that a country's electoral system influences parties' coalition formation has inspired many authors working on the post-industrial welfare state.

Still, electoral systems do not affect an actor's first-order preferences, only their ability to pursue them. Preferences are, like veto points, exogenous. It is the case, moreover, that the choice of electoral system is probably endogenous to the modernization process and the associated welfare state development. Although a fierce debate has raged over why some countries opted for proportional representation when others stayed with the first-past-the-post system, the main competing arguments both relate to the factors outlined above. Boix (1999; 2010) draws on Rokkan's historical work and argues that the old bourgeois elite typically accepted proportional representation in the face of a strong and rising labor movement. The choice was basically a precaution against losing power altogether, which would happen if the Social Democratic party, based on a large proportion (but not necessarily the plurality) of votes, won a majority of seats in parliament. In this scenario, it was better to introduce a system in which no party would be able to muster a majority on their own. It is, in other words, no coincidence that it was those countries with the weakest labor movements, above all else the English-speaking settler colonies, that stayed with the first-past-the-post system. Cusack et al. (2007; 2010), in sharp contrast, argue that proportional representation was adopted at the behest of business in coordinated market economies that wanted a party dedicated to serving their interests in negotiations with the labor movement. This can essentially explain the same cross-country pattern as the Boix-Rokkan argument.

To me, however, the takeaway point is simple: No matter what account is correct, the proposed theoretical mechanisms are part and parcel of the modernization process. If proportional representation was chosen because the labor movement was strong, then the electoral system is a result of labor movement strength, just like the welfare state (according to the power resource theory). If proportional representation was chosen because business wanted to ensure a good bargaining climate in coordinated market economies, then the electoral system is a result of self-serving business interests, just like the welfare state (according to the business-centered approach).

Conclusion

I have now made my case for the welfare state literature's labor market bias. In my reading, this bias stems back to the foundational pieces of Polyani (2001 [1944]) and Wilensky and Lebeaux (1958) and has been reproduced ever since. The key moment in the literature is when the risk of unemployment is linked with the popular demand for protection by the welfare state. From then on, virtually all serious theoretical developments are aimed at understanding this connection: What does it mean, exactly, in terms of citizen preferences? How are these transformed into macro-level politics? How has the transition from an industrial to a post-industrial economy affected preferences and politics?

The past few decades of research has made us all much wiser on these issues. What is more, some of the rough edges in the debates between power resource theorists and business-centered scholars have been rounded. Much of today's best work integrates insights from both traditions. I have tried to highlight points of agreement (even when the authors have not done so themselves), of which there are so many that it makes sense to talk of a standard account of the welfare state's development. We now understand that citizens' preferences for protection against labor market risks are a function of both their present income and their desire to hedge against the future loss of that income. We also understand that welfare state politics has gone from being comparably dichotomous with the labor movement, pitched against business—albeit with extensive corporatist bargaining and the religious cleavage modifying the clash in many European countries—to highly fragmented, as new and old labor market groups have regrouped their party loyalties, thus creating room for reforms of unemployment protection, employment security, leave schemes, and so forth. This is all part of the history of the welfare state, but it is only that—a part. It is my job in the rest of this thesis to bring the other part better into view.

Chapter 3
The psychology of social risks

The previous chapter reviewed the labor market bias of the literature. One of the central findings of the chapter was that citizens, according to the literature, are motivated to maximize either their current or future income, or both. This thinking about what motivates people points to two characteristics of the literature that are equally problematic from my perspective. First, and most obviously, people are assumed to be driven by income. This, of course, follows directly from the welfare state literature's labor market bias; the primary utility people get from the labor market *is* income, together with the wealth that such income allows people to accumulate over time. Second, to the extent that the literature even considers how people make up their minds, the assumption is that people can calculate what is best for them through some sort of explicit cognitive reasoning.

This chapter challenges both assumptions. While I have no trouble accepting the received wisdom that people consider their income when they develop preferences about labor market-related welfare state programs, this assumption appears wrongheaded when it comes to those welfare state programs that are aimed at life cycle risks. It seems ludicrous to suggest that maximization of income is the main motive for the sick, infirm, and old. All individuals want to avoid pain and death and the degrading and sometimes lonely lives that are associated with them. No income transfer, no matter how generous, can compensate for a premature or undignified death; the primary utility people get out of good health and happy old age is not money, but exactly that—good health and happy old age.

I also want to challenge the view that people develop a preference by calculating what is best for them. All the micro-level welfare state theories mentioned above adhere to some (soft) version of rational choice theory, when they argue that people use their position in the labor market—typically defined by their skills specificity, income, or job status—to deduce the form of social protection they prefer. Such a simplistic view of human psychology might be sufficient for analyzing preference formation in the domain of the labor market (though probably not). However, it is decidedly inadequate when considering life cycle risks. Life cycle risks are as old as the human species, and therefore have affected the way people reason about them in ways that cannot be captured with any "rational calculus" model alone.

I propose a new perspective on the psychology of social risks that is far more realistic and, I claim, more explanatorily powerful than what is offered by the existing literature. This new perspective draws heavily on well-established insights from mainstream cognitive psychology about so-called Type 1 and Type 2 reasoning (Evans 2008; Stanovich 2011; Evans and Stanovich 2013). Type 1 is the umbrella term for a set of mental processes that do not require working memory and that function autonomously, that is, without explicit cognition. The mental processes of Type 1 reasoning frequently take the form of "intuitions" that evolved early in human, or even pre-human, history to deal with specific problems and then, over the course of millennia, became hardwired into the human brain. Type 2 reasoning, conversely, requires working memory and is associated with conscious, consequential decision-making of the sort envisioned by the existing welfare state literature. This type of reasoning broadly corresponds to Béland and Cox's (2011: 3-4) definition of ideas as causal beliefs. In the context of my model, we can, therefore, think of Type 1 reasoning as *intuitions* and Type 2 reasoning as *ideas*.

The fact that life cycle risks are an ingrained feature of human existence, whereas labor market risks are very recent in the context of evolutionary history, is significant in several ways. First, people's *cost perceptions* are different across the two areas, with life cycle risks evoking much stronger negative feelings than labor market risks. Second, people's *deservingness perceptions* are different too. People tend to feel much more compassionate about those exposed to life cycle risks, as opposed to labor market risks. Third, for these reasons, opinions about the need for life cycle risk protection tend to be much less flexible than opinions about labor market risk protection. Still, while opinions about the need for life cycle risk protection tend to be inflexible, opinions about proper policy solutions are not. That is, although people have strong intuitions about the need for protection against life cycle risks, they have no similar intuitions about how precisely to provide that protection. This opens the door for considerable policy engineering by elite political actors.

Now, a critical reader might object to my argument that loss of income can also affect a person's health (though of course not old age and its ultimate outcome). Does that not imply that the distinction between labor market and life cycle risks is smaller than I suggest? Are the old theories in fact enough for analyzing life cycle risks? There are several reasons why this is not the case. First, the scholars reviewed in Chapter 3 never suggest that their focus on income is a stand-in or proxy for something more profound or dangerous such as, for example, failing health. In this narrow sense, it is obvious that we cannot rely solely on the existing work, but, as a minimum, must seriously review its foundational assumptions.

Second, although it is true that going without an income can cause starvation and even death, this does not mean that the two risk types are identical. Physical discomfort is a secondary, or derived, effect of labor market risks that may or may not follow from a loss of income. Social networks like the family and local community, together with public social assistance schemes, normally function as a safety net between joblessness and starvation. In the developed world, able-bodied individuals are very rarely allowed to die from hunger because they cannot find a job. This does not mean that income loss cannot have adverse effects on a range of other outcomes—from political participation over social mobility to some health-related conditions—but it does mean that equating income loss with threats to individuals' physical integrity is far too simplistic.

Third, individuals can simultaneously belong to two risk categories. In the event an unemployed person also becomes sick from, for example, malnutrition, he enters the life cycle risk category, triggering a set of powerful psychological responses within himself and those around him. As a result, the now-sick unemployed person will be viewed much more favorably by the public than when he was merely unemployed. If income loss was linked intimately with threats against physical integrity in the minds of ordinary people, as a protagonist of the existing literature might suggest, clearly there ought to be no differences between the two risk types regarding psychological mechanisms and policy preferences. There are, but the existing literature simply has no way of accounting for them. For that, we need a model that links the different risk types with different modes of reasoning. This is precisely what I provide in this chapter.

In the rest of this chapter, I go through the motions of outlining this argument and what more exactly it implies. My ambition, as stated, is to offer a new perspective on the psychology of social risks

that is better able to account for how the welfare
state is organized, as well as its underlying political
processes. In the next section, I discuss in detail
what life cycle risks are and how they differ from labor market risks. I also elaborate when a risk can be
said to be social. Some of what I have to say here will
be shockingly self-explanatory to normal people, but
brand new to welfare state scholars. In the following
two sections, I then present the thesis' argument on
the psychology of social risks.

Two types of risks

Risk is defined as the likelihood of an event multi-
plied by the cost if the event occurs. Risks come in
all shapes and forms, but only some become the subject of communal intervention. According to Esping-
Andersen (1999: 37), risks become "social" for three
reasons: first, if there are collective consequences
of the risk suffered by individuals; second, as the increasing complexity of society creates risks that are
outside the control of individuals; and third, because
society recognizes them as meriting public action.
The first two reasons follow from the modernization
process. Anticipating Iversen and Soskice (2001),
Esping-Andersen observes that labor market protection is often a precondition for workers to behave
economically efficiently:

If, for example, people without social security risk unemployment, they are more likely to resist any kind of technological change that would augment that risk.

In other words, risks are something governments and other collective actors engage with when the economy would otherwise be in jeopardy. This, basically, is the risk socialization process imagined by Katzenstein (1985), Swenson (2002), and Mares (2003) when they argue that governments and business interests use expansive welfare state arrangements to optimize the economy. In comparison, the third reason stands out due to its almost tautological formulation: a risk becomes a social risk if society thinks that it should. This reflects the fact that some social risks have no obvious relevance for economic efficiency but have been recognized as warranting society's attention. From the perspective of the existing welfare state literature, the main route to such recognition, apart from economic efficiency, is the pressure from disadvantaged groups as envisioned by the power resource theory and newer coalitional models. In this scenario, representatives of the disadvantaged have been able to push through social protection, effectively turning individual risks into social ones by brute legislative force.

Underlying the notion of social risks outlined here is also an implicit understanding not just of the source of those risks, the modernization process, but also its manifestation—namely loss of income.

To see how closely linked the two are—and how pervasive the influence of Polyani (2001 [1944]) and Wilensky and Lebeaux (1958) is—consult Esping-Andersen (1999: 37), where "survival itself" is equated with having a job:

> *Dependency on market income is a primary catalyst of generalized risks because survival itself is at the mercy of conditions over which individuals have little say; markets cannot guarantee an income, nor a job. Because market economies are dynamic, workers may find themselves technologically redundant; because they are competitive, the less endowed may find themselves marginalized. Mass unemployment is a phenomenon unique to wage-earner societies.*

The equation between social risks and income loss is abundant in the literature, as detailed in the last chapter. Apart from Esping-Andersen (1999), Moene and Wallerstein (2001), Iversen and Soskice (2001), Rehm (2011; 2016), Gingrich and Ansell (2012), and Alt and Iversen (2017), all propose theories that explicitly emphasize this equation, but many more rely on it more or less implicitly. All of this makes perfect sense when studying the effects of the modernization process. However, when considering other sources of risk, it becomes much more problematic.

Life cycle risks are defined as risks that stem from human biology and which threaten the physical integrity of individuals.[7] Physical integrity may, in turn, be defined as freedom from ailment, pain, and death. The principal categories of life cycle risks are sickness, injury, and old age. Childbirth and child-rearing are latent life cycle risks because they only potentially threaten the mother or child's physical integrity; luckily most births and upbringings happen without these threats ever being realized. Sickness, injury, and old age are, by contrast, defined as currently being in a state of ailment or pain. The World Health Organization (2015: 25) defines aging as

> *the gradual accumulation of a wide variety of molecular and cellular damage. Over time, this damage leads to a gradual decrease in physiological reserves, an increased risk of many diseases, and a general decline in the capacity of the individual. Ultimately, it will result in death.*

7   The term 'life cycle risks' is lifted from Esping-Andersen (1999: 41). However, to him these risks are, as always, just a matter of having too low an income. As he notes, "The life cycle of poverty is closely associated with the lack of correspondence between age-specific needs and earnings: young families have costly needs and low income, earnings rise later on (when children have left), and then they decline sharply in old age."

To the World Health Organization, the increased risk of sickness is one of the defining characteristics of aging. Still, sickness and, for that matter, injury are tricky concepts. Both are so associated with ailment and pain that defining the terms is almost impossible due to circularity (Boyd 2000). Consulting dictionaries, one mostly finds a list of synonyms. Merriam-Webster defines sickness as ill health, illness, or a specific disease, whereas injury is defined as an act that damages or hurts.[8] That said, the common core of all these synonyms appears to be that sickness is a malfunctioning of the body's normal homeostatic processes, while injury is a damage to the body caused by external forces. While sounding more precise, these definitions are also mainly circular (what is "malfunctioning" and "damage" if not exactly sickness and injury, respectively?).

That sickness and injury are at the same time both so hard to define and universally recognizable hints at a fundamental point: the absence of them is regarded as an ultimate goal, impossible to motivate or justify further. Aging is different in this respect for two reasons. First, it only increases the propensity for sickness; it does not imply that people actually are sick. Second, aging is a process that occurs throughout life. Everybody ages from the hour they are born to the day they die. This means

8   This is also true if one adheres to the expansive definition in the World Health Organization's 1948 constitution: "Health is a state of complete physical, mental and social well-being and not merely the absence of disease or infirmity." Apart from disease and infirmity still featuring without a proper definition, well-being is now added to the circular mix.

that while aging is a source of threats to the physical integrity of individuals, we need to differentiate between those periods of life when aging is a big risk ("old age") and those periods when it is a small risk. The point at which old age sets in varies greatly across individuals and conditions, but at a certain point in people's lives, aging-based threats will have augmented so substantially that the majority of ailments and deaths stems from them (World Health Organization 2015: 26):

> *With increasing age, numerous underlying physiological changes occur, and the risk of chronic disease rises. By age 60, the major burdens of disability and death arise from age-related losses in hearing, seeing and moving, and noncommunicable diseases, including heart disease, stroke, chronic respiratory disorders, cancer and dementia.*

So, while aging per se should not be considered a life cycle risk, old age should. From a conceptual perspective, another important issue is the probability distribution of old age. The risk of old age, as defined by the World Health Organization, in fact consists of two parts. The first is an increased likelihood of becoming sick; the other is a general decline of physiological reserves and capabilities. Whereas the former part implies a probability of less than one, the latter implies a probability of exactly one (that is, it is predetermined). All people, unless they die prematurely, will suffer this general decline and eventually perish, yet only some old people will become severely sick in the process.

The composite nature of the risk of old age highlights how the likelihood of events may not be identical across different forms of life cycle risks. However, while the probability of an event can vary, the costs when it does occur are uniformly high. No matter if we are dealing with severe sickness, major injury, age-related loss of physical and mental abilities, or death, these sorts of physical integrity infringements arguably rate as some of the worst things individuals will ever experience. Although no hard data exist on this, I believe it is a fair assumption to make. Inspired by Maslow's (1943) hierarchy of needs, I believe, moreover, that it is reasonable to assume that people generally value their physical integrity more highly than their current and future income. If not, people would accept a monetary reward in return for getting, for instance, lung cancer, dementia, or a stroke. Even if the reward were enormous, such a proposition appears implausible. I return to the issue of cost perceptions further below.

There is a final distinction between sickness and injury, on the one hand, and old age, on the other, which should be discussed. This is the *plasticity of needs assessment*. While there is no doubt that old age is a core life cycle risk, the point at which an individual is considered old varies according to their appearance and personality, as well as social norms. Some may be considered old when turning 60, others only when reaching 70. Deciding when someone is sick or injured is, in contrast, much less negotiable. These varying degrees of plasticity probably flow from the fact that sickness and injury normally occur as single, manifest events (accidents, infections, etc.), whereas old age gradually emerges as a natural process over a period of several years. The abruptness of change makes sickness and injury far easier to spot. However, from the perspective of my argument, the plasticity of needs assessment is interesting, but not crucial. The key point is that *when* people are considered old, they are regarded by themselves and others as belonging to a special, high-risk category.

For the reasons outlined so far, life cycle risks constitute a risk type that is distinct from labor market risks. First, the source of the risks is different. One flows from the biology of human beings, the other from the modernization process. Second, the entity at risk is distinct. Life cycle risks pose a threat to individuals' physical integrity, while labor market risks threaten individuals' current and future income. Third, the cost suffered by individuals from severe life cycle events is greater than the cost from severe labor market events.

As mentioned in this chapter's introduction, I am not arguing that a loss of income cannot eventually lead to a situation where the jobless face starvation and even death. However, this is derived from the primary effect, namely lost income. In developed societies, the connection between unemployment and starvation is weak. This is not to belittle the fact that many families in Europe and North America are unable to afford the food they want (Dugan and Wendt 2014), but people's physical integrity is normally not at stake. It is also true that there is a socio-economic gradient in many health-related conditions (but not, of course, in old age) because people with a lower income tend to have different lifestyles from people with higher incomes (Marmot 2005; Mackenbach et al. 2008; Elo 2009; Meara et al. 2017).

But this points to a major puzzle: While there is a socio-economic gradient in some health-related risks, there is virtually no gradient in people's preferences for health protection (Jensen 2014; Jensen and Petersen 2017; see also Chapter 4). This stands in stark contrast to the findings in the extant literature, as detailed in the last chapter. Here people's socio-economic position maps onto their preferences, but no similar pattern exists for health. People reason about health care *as if* there were no socio-economic gradient. Crucially, there is nothing in the literature to suggest why people should reason differently about health-related risks and labor market risks. If people are maximizing life cycle risk protection in the same way as they are assumed to maximize labor market risk protection, we should see, at least for health care, a different pattern of public preferences from the one we do. To solve the puzzle, we need a new model of the psychology of social risks. To be convincing, such a model should be able to account not only for the puzzle of uniformly high support for health care, but also more generally for the differences between people's reasoning about life cycle and labor market risks. I spend the rest of the chapter outlining such a model.

Ideas and intuitions: The basic distinction

The welfare state literature is characterized not just by an emphasis on the role of current or future income as the motivational driver of citizens but also by its reliance on (some soft version of) rational choice as its model of how citizens make up their minds. Depending on the exact setup of the theory, citizens are assumed to rely on their position in society's income or risk distributions to deduce their preferred policies.[9] These are rather taxing assumptions. Barber IV et al. (2013) show that even in a laboratory setting with full information about each participant's income and risk exposure, people are unable to differentiate between income and insurance motives. This undercuts much of the literature even before we get to the issue of whether people know about their position in the income and risk distributions.

As mentioned previously, I rely on the well-established distinction between Type 1 and Type 2

---

9   In the welfare state literature, rational choice has gotten a bad name as being overly simplistic. Still, it is striking that the only models of welfare state development that explicitly integrate the micro and macro level virtually all rely on rational choice arguments (e.g., Moene and Wallerstein 2001; Iversen and Soskice 2001). Other approaches like the power resource theory simply dodge the issue of how voters think.

reasoning (Evans 2008; Stanovich 2011; Evans and Stanovich 2013). The former is defined as mental processes that occur without the employment of working memory, whereas the latter is mental processes that require working memory. In the context of my argument, the key feature of Type 1 reasoning is that these processes frequently take the form of evolutionary-based intuitions, while Type 2 reasoning takes the form of explicit cognitive calculations. The capacity of working memory is highly limited, meaning that this type of reasoning tends to be slow. Type 2 reasoning roughly parallels Béland and Cox's (2011) definition of ideas as causal beliefs, which is why I label the two types of mental processes *intuitions* and *ideas*.[10] Highlighting the correspondence between Type 2 reasoning and ideas also allows me to link my argument better with the extant welfare state literature.

Viewing ideas as causal belief implies three things (Béland and Cox 2011: 3-4):

> *First, as beliefs, ideas are products of cognition. They are produced in our minds and are connected to the material world only via our interpretations of our surroundings. [...] Second, as causal beliefs, ideas posit connections between things and between people in the world. [...] Finally, causal beliefs, or ideas, provide guides for action. Ideas help us to think about ways to*

10   Kahneman and Frederick (2002) also label Type 1 reasoning 'intuitions'.

address problems and challenges that we face
and therefore are the cause of our actions.

The key issue at stake here is that people base their decisions on beliefs about what their actions will achieve. An idea may be wrong or right; what matters is that people act on it as if it were right. Most of the time, ideas about salient political and social realities such as the welfare state will not be entirely inaccurate, but the potential errors can be big. Bartels (2005), in a famous study from the US, for instance, shows how most Americans were unable to link Bush's 2003 tax cuts with rising inequality and their own redistributive pre-dispositions. This is also manifest in the findings of Barber IV et al. (2013) that even after receiving all the necessary pieces of information to form opinions along the lines of the theoretically sophisticated welfare state literature, people prove unable to do so.

The reason for this lack of accuracy stems from the limited capacity of individuals' working memory, which severely constrains the mental resources available to take in and evaluate all the necessary information. People are bounded rational. This implies that they are unable to foresee in any great detail the consequences of their decisions, unlikely to ascribe the correct values to the consequences, and incapable of assessing all possible alternatives before making a decision (Simon 1997 [1945]: 92-97; Jones 2001: 34-48). As a result, an individual may develop ideas that are either wrong or work against that person's material interests.

It is important to realize, though, that just because people fail to develop correct causal beliefs about the notoriously complicated American tax system, or in the artificial setting of a lab, their causal beliefs are not wholly random either. One reason for this is, as emphasized by Jones (2001: 54-56, 63-64), that people try to get their ideas correct; they are intendedly rational. Objectively correct ideas will often be more helpful when trying to get what you want than incorrect ones. So, even though people never approach full rationality, they might learn enough to get by in a process of so-called satisficing.

Intended rationality is made easier by the fact that people form their ideas in social networks, which help correct some of the worst misunderstandings individuals might entertain. However, because people self-select into social networks based on their family background, education, workplace experience, and so forth (McPherson et al. 2001), there are limits to this corrective mechanism. Social networks, in fact, tend to crystalize ideas around specific common narratives or ideologies (Huckfeldt and Sprague 1987; Huckfeldt et al. 1993; Visser and Mirabile 2004). Mosimann and Pontusson (2017), for instance, argue that unions help their members produce consistent policy preferences by disseminating factual knowledge and distributive norms via the workplace. One might imagine similar processes taking place in workplaces more broadly (Kitschelt and Rehm 2014), as well as the educational system

(Stubager 2008). Social networks, in short, narrow the number of viable ideas to a few competing ones that then help individual members of these networks to structure their beliefs and preferences.

The existence and persistence of social networks, many of which last for long periods of time, explain why it is not surprising that welfare state preferences are often fairly well-structured. Individuals with a low income are typically more supportive of redistribution than high-income individuals, just as members of the working class are more supportive than members of the upper class. However, these connections between socio-economic positions and concrete policy preferences are often not deduced by citizens but adopted via socialization in social networks like the school system and the workplace, where opinion leaders such as older students, teachers, and union representatives set the tone. With time, such socialization creates a logic of appropriateness where a causal belief is imbued with a normative value independent of its concrete content (March and Olson 1989: 21-38).

The limited capacity of the working memory also means that people's attention span is restricted (Jones 2001: 15). Most of the time, people do not think about the welfare state. It typically requires some sort of prominent problem or event for people to direct their attention to an issue, for example news stories about benefit fraud or overly long waiting lists (Baumgartner and Jones 1993: 103-125; Kingdon 1995: 90-98). One implication of this is potentially dramatic swings in attention as an issue stops being ignored and instead gets the full attention of the people and, by implication, the organizations people inhabit (Jones and Baumgartner 2005). Another implication is that since people hold distinct ideas, they will interpret information about problems differently. An individual's notions of how to solve a problem depend on the causal beliefs they have about the world and how rooted they are (Kingdon 1995: 109-113, 139-142; Stone 2011: 207-218).

Because ideas filter information about problems, they quite frequently narrow the set of possible policy responses to a few that correspond with actors' preexisting causal beliefs and the norms that have developed along with them (Kunda 1990; Baumgartner and Jones 1993: 25-38; Hall 1993; Blyth 2002: 35-44; Leeper and Slothuus 2014). Ideas thus become cognitive locks that neutralize the disruptive effect of newly emerged problems. This is due partly to the vested interests that are sustained by the presence of an underlying idea, and who will go to great lengths to argue for its continuing merit. However, ideas are, at any rate, often flexible enough to suffer a fair amount of stretching or post hoc rationalization. Only when anomalies have accumulated critically, and new, plausible ideas are available, will people update from one to the other. In the context of citizens' welfare state preferences, these sorts of updates will be very rare. Ideas are overwhelmingly a force of stability.

Intuitions are different from ideas because they affect preferences without involving people's working memory. Intuition-based decision-making is fast, automatic, and independent of cognitive abilities. As Stanovich (2011: 19) puts it, executing intuition-based decisions "is mandatory when their triggering stimuli are encountered, and they do not depend on higher-level control systems." Many collectively shared intuitions are rooted in mental processes that have been with the human species forever, or date even further back to our hominid ancestors (Evans 2008: 259-261).[11] Think of the knee-jerk fear reaction individuals have when confronted with snakes. Here, the snake is the stimuli that automatically—that is, without a deliberate decision—makes us highly alert.

A core insight of evolutionary psychology is to highlight how evolutionarily evolved intuitions can structure modern-day individuals' decision-making, even though the environment that first gave cause to the intuition has disappeared (Tooby and Cosmides 1992). For instance, Sell et al. (2009a; 2010) show that people can assess males' physical strength from photographs and recordings of male voices, while Nguyen et al. (2017) finds that physically stronger participants in anonymous auction games tend to win more often than physically weaker participants. Resonating with this, Sell et al. (2009b) shows that stronger males are more supportive of military force in international conflicts. The development

11   I emphasize collectively shared intuitions because some intuitions are strictly private. A gifted piano player can perform without the use of working memory, but the intuition is private and disappears with the individual.

of such behavior is difficult to explain without an evolutionary perspective, and researchers assume that it served some function back in human pre-history even though it would appear irrelevant or even counter-productive today.

Ideas and intuitions about life cycle and labor market risks

The previous section outlined the basic distinction between ideas and intuitions. Now, I want to link these two decision-making modes with the two types of risks that were introduced earlier. In a nutshell, my argument boils down to the following: In the domain of life cycle risks, there exist powerful intuitions that determine cost perceptions ("how dangerous is this to me?") as well as deservingness perceptions ("how deserving are the needy of help?"). These intuitions mean that support for life cycle risk protection will be uniformly high everywhere. In the domain of labor market risks, no similar intuitions exist, entailing that support for labor market risk protection is much more open to the social construction of ideas by elite actors (also known as framing). Across both domains, however, no intuitions have evolved about how to provide protection concretely, allowing elite actors to pitch specific policy solutions.

As a first step, it is necessary to consider how risks, per se, feature in human decision-making. The welfare state literature, as already detailed, assumes that individuals will evaluate risks using explicit cognitive reasoning to determine cold-mindedly how they should act on a risk. This consequentialist approach stands in contrast to what Loewenstein et al. (2001) call the risk-as-feelings approach, which draws on well-established psychological research and mirrors the dual-process model presented above. In this framework (ibid.: 270),

> *Responses to risky situations (including decision-making) result in part from direct (i.e., not cortically mediated) emotionally influences, including feelings such as worry, fear, dread, or anxiety. People are assumed to evaluate risky alternatives at a cognitive level, as in traditional models, based largely on the probability and desirability of associated consequences. [...] At the same time, however, feeling states are postulated to respond to factors, such as the immediacy of a risk, that do not enter into cognitive evaluations of the risks and also respond to probabilities and outcome values in a fashion that is different from the way these variables enter into cognitive evaluations.*

While leaving room for intendedly rational calculations, the key message is that people will often be overcome by negative feelings. Basic emotions like fear flow from intuitions (i.e., they are mental processes that do not require working memory to operate), and dealing with basic emotions tends to crowd out all other actions (Loewenstein 1996; Evans and Stanovich 2013: 225, 236). Loewenstein et al. (2001) point to two factors that, from the perspective of my argument, are particularly likely to trigger powerful emotional responses. First, the vividness of the risk. The more vivid a risk appears, the more likely people are to base their decision-making on feelings. Here, the nature of life cycle risks as compared to labor market risks becomes important. Sickness, pain, and death and everything that goes with them simply create more vivid mental images than losing one's job. This does not imply that joblessness cannot be framed as something dramatic and unpleasant, but such a framing requires additional information (i.e., the frame) about the situation of the job seeker. In contrast, even neutral statements like "John has dementia" or "Sarah has been involved in a car acci- dent" bring forth vivid associations. In part, this is because of the impersonal nature of labor markets and economies themselves, where causes are nor- mally aggregate and abstract (e.g., a downturn or globalization); these are phenomena that cannot be seen with one's own eyes. This, in turn, harks back to and reinforces the proposition that the (non-mon- etary) costs of life cycle risks are bigger than the (monetary) costs of labor market risks.

The second trigger is evolutionary prepar- edness. For some risks, humans have evolved in- tuitions about the danger that set off feelings of fear or anxiety when we encounter the triggering stimuli. Take the snake example from above, where the snake (the stimuli) triggers a feeling of fear that is entirely automatic. Crucially, Loewenstein et al. (2001: 279) observe,

> *People are likely to react with little fear to certain types of objectively dangerous stimuli that evolution has not prepared them for, such as guns, hamburgers, automobiles, smoking, and unsafe sex, even when they recognize the threat at a cognitive level. Types of stimuli that people are evolutionary prepared to fear, such as caged spiders, snakes, or heights (when adequate safety measures are in place), evoke a visceral response even when, at a cognitive level, they are recognized as harmless.*

The fact that threats to individuals' physical integrity are an inseparable part of human history is, in short, another reason to suspect that we have developed fear-based intuitive responses to life cycle risks. This does not imply, of course, that people cannot feel anxiety when risking unemployment. However, it does imply that these feelings will not stem from deep-seated, evolutionary intuitions about danger. Put differently, all serious instances of life cycle risks that people experience are likely to trigger major, negative feelings, automatically (fear of dying, anxiety about getting old and frail, etc.), while feelings concerning labor market risks are much less predetermined.

In summary, the nature of life cycle risks and the psychology of risk evaluation in combination enhance the costs people think they will suffer from life cycle risks, relative to labor market risks. However, our psychological makeup affects not only perceptions of costs but also whether people believe others are deserving of help.[12] In a nutshell, people exposed to life cycle risks are viewed as deserving because humans have developed an intuition that people facing threats to their physical integrity do not have control over their situation. Because labor market risks are so new by evolutionary standards, no similar intuition has emerged for this category of risks. This means that the assessment of whether the jobless and the poor have control over their situation is much more open to interpretation based on people's ideas.

Deservingness perceptions are well documented as affecting support for the welfare state. If an individual believes that the typical recipient of benefits is underserving, he will also be less likely to think that the welfare state ought to provide benefits in the first place. Van Oorschot (2000) shows that deservingness perceptions largely reflect perceptions of control. People in control of their situation (e.g., those who can work but refuse to—the lazy) are regarded as undeserving, while people without con-

12   The basic thrust of this thread of the argument comes from collaborative work with Michael Bang Petersen, although I speculate here on the full range of life cycle risks, not just sickness, as in Jensen and Petersen (2017).

trol (e.g., those who would like to work but cannot—the unlucky) are regarded as deserving.

A new strand of research has linked these deservingness perceptions to our evolutionary past by arguing that strong negative emotional responses to laziness helped our hunter-gatherer ancestors to share resources while avoiding cheaters (Petersen 2012; Petersen et al. 2012). In the context of hunter-gatherer communities, resource-sharing is vital as a way of ensuring against bad luck, such as injuries during hunts and bad weather or wildfires destroying food sources. Even with resource-sharing, hunter-gatherers lived on the edge of survival, but primitive social insurances created a buffer that could make the difference between life and death. For resource-sharing to work, however, people needed to be able to detect cheaters who planned to enjoy the resources collected by others without reciprocating. Over time, this led to the evolution of deservingness intuitions and the strong emotional reactions associated with them. The needy who showed signs of failure to reciprocate (the lazy but in control) evoked feelings of anger, while the needy exhibiting willingness to reciprocate (the unlucky, without control) evoked feelings of compassion.

Life cycle risks are special in the sense that individuals exposed to these risks are almost always considered to be without control over their situation. This is true even in modern-day societies, where sickness and injury do come with a socio-economic gradient reflecting variation between classes in lifestyle choices such as smoking, diet, and exercise (Marmot 2005; Mackenbach et al. 2008; Elo 2009; Meara et al. 2017). The reason lies in the fact that virtually all these lifestyle conditions that now plague society did not exist when our deservingness intuitions evolved. The conditions that people did suffer from—lacerations, infections, and stings— were randomly distributed across the social hierarchy (Kaplan et al. 2000; Sugiyama and Chacon 2000; Sugiyama 2004), which, at any rate, was much flatter then than later on (Flannery and Marcus 2012). Because our intuitions about sickness and injury evolved before the socio-economic gradient, people still intuitively think about these risks in terms of randomness and, hence, as something beyond the control of individuals.

Whereas sickness and injury in hunter-gatherer communities were random events, old age, except in the case of premature death, was predetermined. All humans without exception aged and died. Both randomness and predetermination deprived people of control over their own situations. Of course, old age is still predetermined today, but the fact that it is a biological feature of human existence means that people are likely to have evolved deservingness intuitions about the risk, inducing strong feelings of compassion toward the elderly. Essentially, these automatic feelings of compassion help explain why old people are consistently considered highly deserving of public assistance (cf. van Oorschot 2006; Petersen et al. 2011).

It follows from this that deservingness perceptions related to labor market risks are different from those associated with life cycle risks. First, the modernization process is so recent, and evolution takes so long, that it is unlikely that any collectively shared intuitions have had time to emerge. Second, throughout the short existence of labor market risks, a strong socio-economic gradient in risk exposure has been present. This divide between the haves and the have-nots is indeed a core part of the political history of labor market risks, as described by Polyani (2001 [1944]), Stephens (1979), Korpi (1983), and many other welfare state scholars.

The lack of deep-seated intuitions means that deservingness perceptions are open to the social construction of ideas, while the socio-economic gradient means that the dominant set of ideas that has emerged follows the economic cleavage in society. In the domain of labor market risks, conservatives are likely to ascribe need to laziness, while left-leaning individuals are likely to ascribe need to misfortune. These diverse narratives of deservingness flourish because people do not share any deep intuitions about labor market risks and because citizens are nested in social networks that map onto the socio-economic gradient, aligning the respective deservingness perceptions with people's material self-interests. Working class members are taught by their unions, and tell themselves, that unemployment is caused by structural factors outside their control. Lawyers, engineers, and other high-end private service employees are told by their representatives, and tell themselves, that unemployment is caused by the lack of willpower among the working class. For both groups, their respective causal beliefs are convenient truths that have morphed into norms.

So far, I have argued that life cycle and labor market risks are different from each other due to the ingrained intuitions associated with the former compared to the latter. These are powerful forces in public opinion formation. However, people's preferences in the domain of life cycle risks are not just a function of their collectively shared intuitions, because while we have strong intuitions about the costs of life cycle risks and the deservingness of claimants, there are no similar intuitions about the appropriate solutions. The need for protection against life cycle risks is as old as the human species, but the way of providing this protection is not. This is, at least in part, because of the modernization process, which, especially in the cases of sickness and injury, has hugely expanded the available treatments and the organizational capacity of society. Today we have modern-style hospitals (i.e., where patients are treated, not just kept and cared for) and a highly innovative medical industry, but a hundred years ago both of these were just emerging (Porter 1997).

The consequence is that ideas matter a lot when it comes to suitable solutions for handling life cycle risks. As with labor market risks, people tend to form their ideas about the best way to deal with life cycle risks in social networks. Here, they are influenced by opinion leaders and their own peers, and strong norms can develop about what is appropriate and what is not. However, compared to labor market risks, there are clear constraints on the type of ideas that are viable because they cannot conflict with people's intuitions about costs and deservingness. As a minimum, ideas must be presented as aligning with intuitions, or they will fail to gain traction.

Conclusion

The purpose of this chapter was to challenge two of the main assumptions of the welfare state literature: that people are driven by current or future income and that they evaluate risk using some form of rational calculus. These assumptions are not wrong in the sense that they are never correct. People undoubtedly care about money, and most of us think long and hard about how to maximize or protect it. The point is, however, that money is a much more relevant entity in the domain of labor market risks than in the domain of life cycle risks, and that people seldom rely on rational calculations—especially when it comes to life cycle risks. In a sense, these are trivial observations. However, it is far from trivial to decide what to do about them.

I have tried to draw the contours of a positive analytical framework of how voters in today's welfare states reason. I relied on well-established research on dual processes, bounded rationality, and evolutionary psychology. Although new to the welfare state literature, there is nothing fanciful or far-fetched about my argument (though it may still be wrong, of course). With this psychological model of social risks at hand, I shall highlight a few points that become important in analyzing the politics of life cycle risks in the next chapter.

First, people everywhere are equipped with intuitions that make them fearful of life cycle risks and compassionate toward those exposed to these risks. This does not mean that these intuitions alone decide how people think about these risks. Ideas matter too, and can override intuitions. However, because people always rely on intuitions, if they have any, for their default response, this will be a rather rare occurrence. Second, for labor market risks the picture is practically the reverse. Here, we are stripped of collectively shared intuitions that prime us toward feeling strong emotions when we encounter risks. Instead, socially constructed ideas shape opinions. These ideas will typically be stable because they fit the socio-economic cleavage well, but will not be immutable. Over time, the modal thinking about the causes of labor market risks can shift in ways that are less likely in the domain of life cycle risks.

Chapter 4
The politics
of the welfare state
revisited

The argument of the previous chapter was that life cycle and labor market risks are underpinned by distinct psychological mechanisms. This chapter takes this argument as its starting point and asks how this structures the politics of the welfare state. As explained in Chapter 1, I propose a dual risk model of the welfare state. I fully recognize the importance of labor market risks and the associated politics, as summarized in the standard account of the welfare state literature (cf. Chapter 2). However, the standard account must be complemented with a new understanding of the politics of life cycle risks.

In the dual risk model, the political process takes the form of a sequence of stages starting at the level of voters and then aggregating up through the political system until it ends with a set of public policies. The underlying claim is that politics go "from the bottom up," meaning that the first stage (the voters) causally affects the second stage (party competition), which causally affects the third stage (public policy-making). If we want to understand the grand architecture of the welfare state, we need an approach that connects the policy outcomes of the welfare state with the major contours of society.

However, the politics of life cycle risks is not determined by the social basis alone. The psychology of social risks allows for the possibility that elite actors can shape political processes and policy outcomes significantly. In the domain of life cycle risks, people have strong intuitions about the costs of risks and the deservingness of claimants, but few opinions about how to deal with the risks more concretely. This means that elite actors can pitch solutions that, on the one hand, fit people's intuitions but, on the other, help the elite actors maximize their self-interest and the interests of those they represent. In other words, because of the strong intuitions around life cycle risks, the menu of solutions is smaller than in the domain of labor market risks, and protection against life cycle risks is almost everywhere better than labor market risk protection. Still, there is considerable variation in how life cycle risk protection is provided.

Stage no. 1: Public preferences[13]

Given the elaborate discussion in Chapter 3, the focus in this section is on how the distinct psycholog-

13   This section draws on *The Right and the Welfare State* (Jensen 2014), *Partivalg og Holdninger til Velfærdsstaten* (Arndt and Jensen 2017), *The Deservingness Heuristic* (Jensen and Petersen 2017), and *Risky Business* (Lee et al. 2019).

ical processes of the two risk types have crystalized into two equally distinct sets of public opinion landscapes. Consider Figure 4.1, which reports survey data on the public's belief that governments have a responsibility to handle a given social problem. The figure is composed of survey data from 41 countries from the European Social Survey (Panel A) and the International Social Survey Programme (Panel B), respectively. This is the largest number of countries for which it is possible to obtain comparable data on public opinions about specific social problems with high-quality, nationally representative samples. The horizontal axis reports the percentage of the public that agrees that it is the government's responsibility to ensure health care for the sick (light blue bars), a decent standard of living for the old (medium blue bars) and the unemployed (black bars). The first two variables represent preferences for life cycle risk protection, while the last represents preferences for labor market risk protection.[14]

14   The wording in the European Social Survey, round 4, from 2008, is: "People have different views on what the responsibilities of governments should or should not be. How much responsibility do you think governments should have to ensure [adequate health care for the sick/a reasonable standard of living for the old/a reasonable standard of living for the unemployed]?" Answers were obtained on an 11-point scale with the endpoints "Governments should not be responsible at all" (0) to "Should be entirely governments' responsibility" (10). Respondents choosing 8 or above were coded as supportive. The wording of the International Social Survey Programme's module on the role of government from 2006 is: "On the whole, do you think it should or should not be the government's responsibility to provide [health care for the sick/a decent standard of living for the old/a decent standard of living for the unemployed]?" The scale had four categories: "Definitely should be"/"Probably should be"/"Probably should not be"/"Definitely should not be." The first two categories are coded as supportive.

Figure 4.1. Public beliefs about government responsibility for the old, sick, and unemployed

Panel A

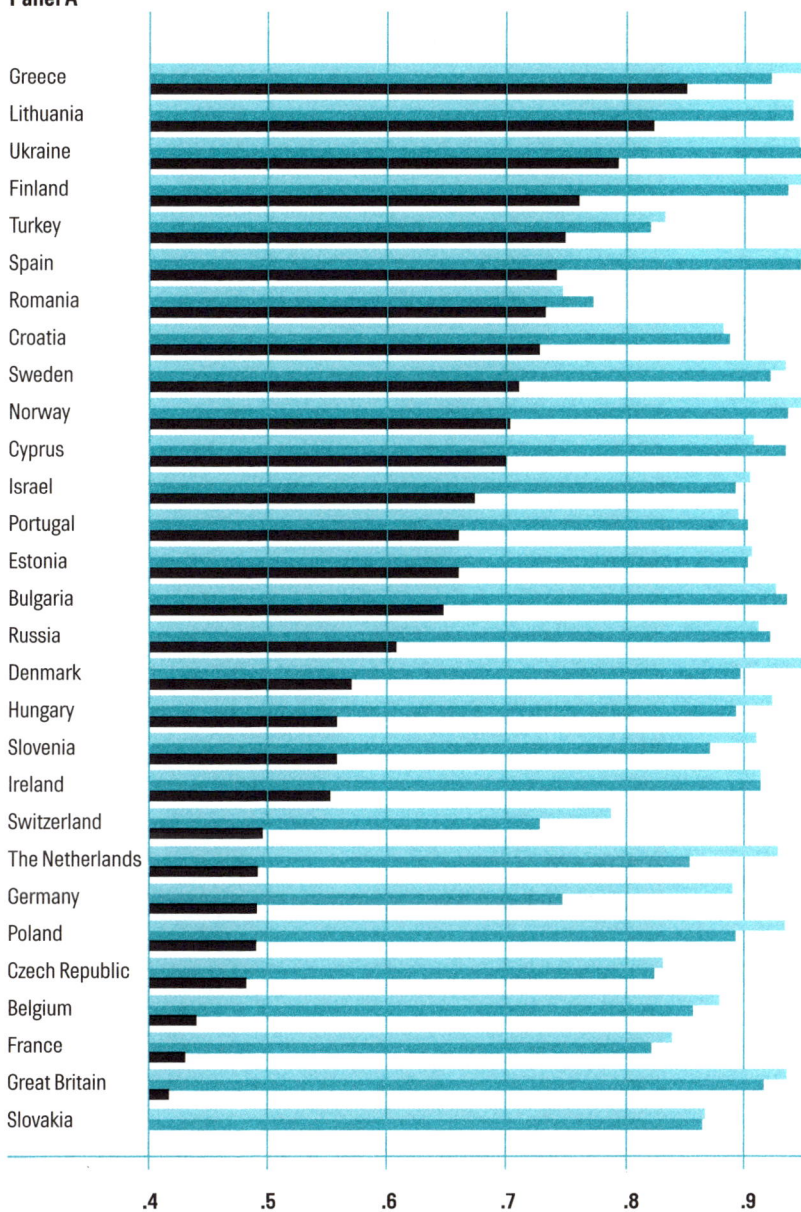

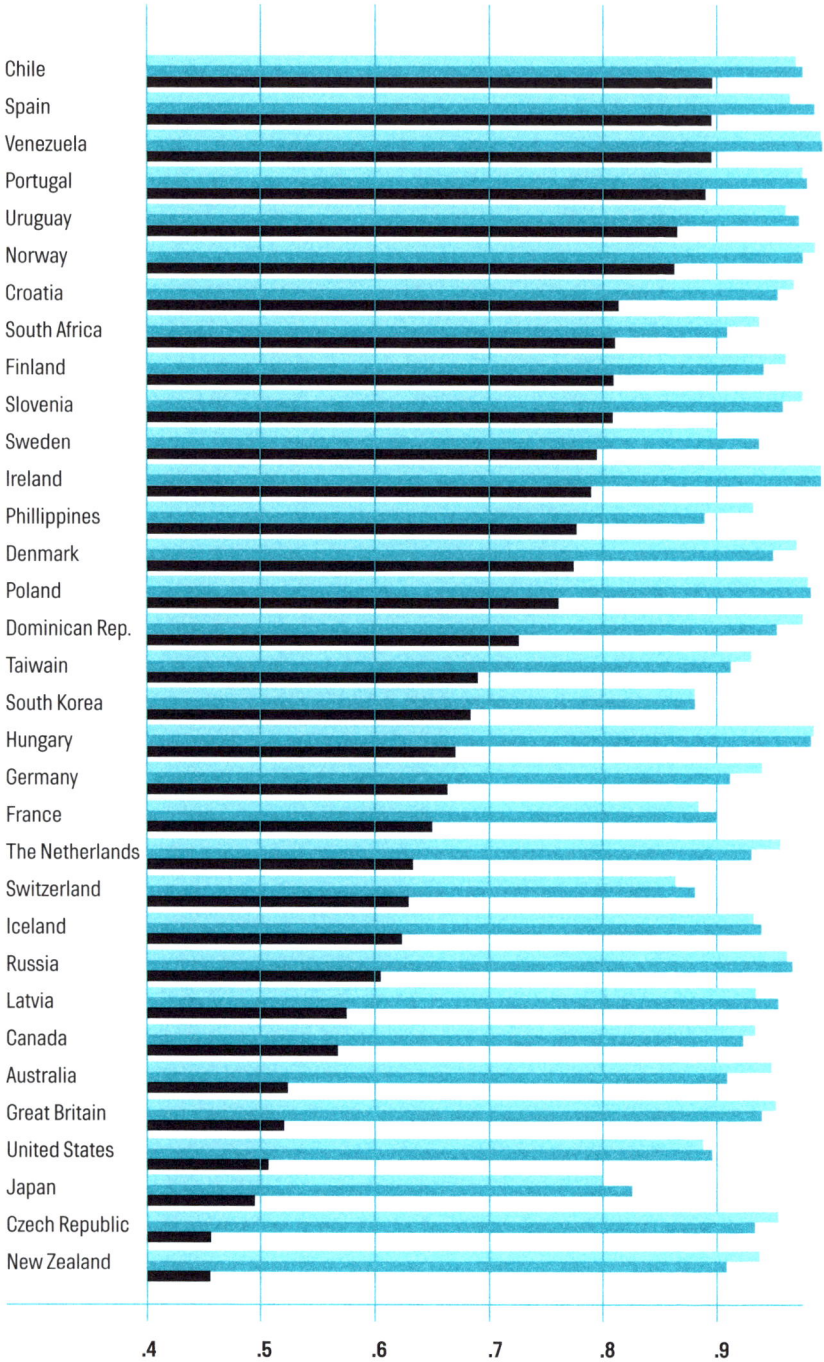

Panel B

Chile	
Spain	
Venezuela	
Portugal	
Uruguay	
Norway	
Croatia	
South Africa	
Finland	
Slovenia	
Sweden	
Ireland	
Phillippines	
Denmark	
Poland	
Dominican Rep.	
Taiwain	
South Korea	
Hungary	
Germany	
France	
The Netherlands	
Switzerland	
Iceland	
Russia	
Latvia	
Canada	
Australia	
Great Britain	
United States	
Japan	
Czech Republic	
New Zealand	

.4   .5   .6   .7   .8   .9

Note: The horizontal axis reports the percentage of the population in a given country that agrees that government has a responsibility to protect the sick (light blue bars), the old (medium blue bars), and the unemployed (black bars). Standard weights have been applied.

Two things are noteworthy. First, overall support is much higher for sickness and old age than for unemployment. Although the exact proportion varies slightly between the two panels because of differences in question-wording, it is evident that massive majorities (typically between 80 and 95 percent of the public) think the government has a responsibility to protect citizens against life cycle risks, whereas support is much more muted when it comes to labor market risks. Second, support is much more uniform for the first two risks than for the last. This matches the argument outlined in the last chapter. Across the globe, people intuitively believe that needs caused by life cycle risks are worthy of support. This, in turn, means that support for government involvement is much less influenced by contextual factors. Beliefs that the government has a responsibility for the jobless is, by comparison, much more amenable to the economic structure of society and the associated social networks on the labor market, leading to much more varied levels of support (as illustrated by Rehm 2011; 2016; Gingrich and Ansell 2012).

The last chapter singled out two underlying reasons for these stark differences, namely the varying cost and deservingness perceptions, respectively, across life cycle and labor market risks. The former relates to individuals' perception of their situation ("How badly am I at risk?"), while the latter relates to individuals' perception of other people's situations ("How deserving are those claiming benefits?").

Unfortunately, there is very little research on cost perceptions and risk types. To amend this, I have collected new survey evidence that allows us to gauge the manifestation of the distinct cost perceptions across life cycle and labor market risks.[15] The main purpose of the survey is to assess a simple but vital assumption in the argument outlined so far: that individuals believe that life cycle risks are worse than labor market risks. One way to get at this is to have the respondents answer this question: "If you had to choose between one of the following two scenarios for the rest of your life, which would you choose?" Based on this prompt, the respondent could then select either "Good health, but no job" or "Bad health, but a secure job."[16] Figure 4.2 summarizes the results. 84 percent opted for the first scenario and only 16 percent for the second. This is quite a strong indication that people tend to view

15   The survey was conducted from January 3 to January 15, 2018, by YouGov, among 1,008 Danes. All respondents were in the workforce and between 18 and 60 years old. The sample is nationally representative in terms of gender, age, geography, and education.
16   For presentational reasons, I chose health as the representation of life cycle risks rather than old age. As discussed in Chapter 3, old age (except for premature death) is ascertained, so the notion that you can select not to become old seems more far-fetched than selecting not to become sick.

risks against their physical integrity as more serious than threats against their income stream.[17]

Figure 4.2. Proportion of the public selecting good/bad health over no/secure job

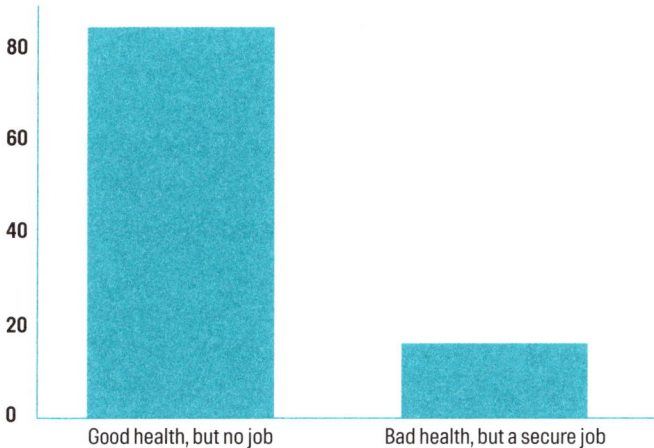

Source: Author's own survey, conducted by YouGov.

We have yet to understand the underlying mechanism of these distinct cost perceptions. In this sense, we know much more about deservingness perceptions, which Michael Bang Petersen and I have explored recently in *The Deservingness Heuristic*. Briefly, what we find is that our respondents *intuitively* view the sick as more lacking in control than the unemployed; that this intuition means

17   I want to emphasize that this does not mean that people do not care about job security. A large majority of European citizens consider employment security an important attribute of a job (Emmenegger 2014: 5). Still, *relative* to life cycle risks, job security pales in importance.

that it is much easier to frame the unemployed as undeserving compared to the sick; that this intuition spills over into greater support for government provision of health care; and that this mechanism appears to exist across national cultures. This, then, is part of the mechanism leading to the well-established observation that the sick (and the old) are regarded as more deserving than the unemployed (e.g., van Oorschot 2006; Petersen et al. 2011).

The structure of cost and deservingness perceptions has a powerful knock-on effect on the public's policy preferences, as already noted. To see what this implies more exactly, we may zoom in on what might be regarded as a conservative case for finding differences between the two risk types, namely Denmark. As suggested by Larsen (2008), the institutional arrangements of the Danish labor market protection system are likely to generate comparably high levels of acceptance among the broader public. While Denmark is an outlier in terms of the generosity of labor market risk protection, it is on the other hand quite typical when it comes to life cycle risk protection, which is no more generous than elsewhere in the developed world (cf. below). This should narrow the gap, all else being equal, between public support for life cycle and labor market risk protection. The differences we locate here are likely to be at least as big, and probably bigger, elsewhere.

The 2015 Danish National Election Study asked a set of questions about whether the government ought to spend more or less on given policy areas. By subtracting the two response categories, we obtain a measure of the majority in favor of more (or less) spending (Arndt and Jensen 2017). By these measures, there is a 69 percent majority for more spending on elderly care, a 66 percent point majority in favor of more spending on health care, and a 43 percent majority in favor of more spending on the basic state pension (*folkepensionen*). These huge majorities should be compared with a much more modest majority of 13 percentage points in favor of more spending on unemployment insurance and an eight-percentage-point majority wanting less spending on social assistance.

There are also noteworthy differences in the partisanship of public support. When it comes to elderly care, health care, and the basic state pension, the supporters of the two mainstream competitors for the government, the Liberal Party (*Venstre*) and the Social Democratic Party, hold equally expansionist opinions. There are even solid majorities in favor of more spending among the supporters of the fiscally conservative Liberal Alliance. There is, in short, no partisan conflict at the voter level in terms of public spending on the two programs protecting against life cycle risks. This should be compared with voter preferences for unemployment insurance and social assistance. Here, large majorities among the voters of both the hawkish Liberal Alliance and more center-right Liberal Party want cuts, whereas the center-left voters favor expansion.

Another interesting case is the US. Given that the US is normally considered a welfare state laggard and "special," it is worth emphasizing that Americans conform to the general picture outlined so far. In Figure 4.1, almost 90 percent believe it is the government's responsibility to ensure adequate health care for the sick and a decent standard of living for the old. Only approximately 50 percent believe the same about the unemployed. The significant support for life cycle risk protection fits other findings from the US. Since 1973, surveys have asked whether Americans felt "too little," "just about right," or "too much" was being spent on improving and protecting the nation's health. In 1973, 61 percent said "too little;" by 2008, that number had increased to 75 percent (Blendon et al. 2011: 59). By 2009, 49 percent said they were willing to pay more to increase the number of Americans with health insurance, while a full 66 percent said providing health care for all Americans is more important than keeping taxes down (ibid.: 125). In 2008, only 6 and 11 percent favored cutting spending on Medicare and Medicaid, respectively. Among self-declared Republicans, 8 and 14 percent, respectively, wanted to cut Medicare and Medicaid (ibid.: 175).

The US is a useful case to exemplify the complex opinion formation processes surrounding life cycle risks. The public unambiguously believes that the government has a role as protector of the sick and the old, a spillover from all humans' intuitions about costs and deservingness. Yet how this should be done is a much more open question, especially for health care. Because of the setup of their political system, Americans have so far been denied a full-blown universal health care system as is de facto found everywhere else in the Western world (Steinmo and Watts 1995; Hacker 2002). Instead, a plethora of schemes has been introduced over the years, which has led to a unique situation. First, an electoral majority in the US has decent—and in many instances better than decent—health care coverage. The US health care system has many downsides in terms of economic costs and lack of proper coverage for millions, but it delivers solid protection to the majority. This means that many Americans have something to lose from reforms, all else being equal, which makes people skeptical of radical change.

Second, health care coverage is mainly organized as publicly subsidized employer insurances. As Mettler (2011) argues, the fact that health care comes via one's job, but heavily subsidized, means that most people are unaware that the government is the sponsor of much of their protection against sickness and injury. People essentially believe that they, together with their employer, are the sole cause of their health care. Government, on the other hand, is viewed as an institution that taxes, but only delivers benefits to the poor (and undeserving). This reinforces a broader ideology of individualism, which ultimately casts the government as bad and private initiative as good. In sum, Americans' gut reaction is to think that everybody should have protection against health risks, but the structure of the existing system means that people shy away from all-out support for government programs as the solution. In the words of Page and Jacobs (2009), Americans are "conservative egalitarians."

The US is a special case in terms of health care, but over the last 50 years or so the country has crawled toward universal health care and is, hence, following exactly the same trajectory as all other countries. Still, while all countries are expanding coverage, they are doing so in different ways. In health care, some have a National Health System, others a pillarized system, and others again a mix (Blank and Burau 2010: 11-17). In pensions, some have tax-financed basic pensions, others a contribution-based savings system, and others a mix (Immergut et al. 2007). Whatever the setup, voters can become highly wedded to the national mode of life cycle protection because this is what they know and feel comfortable with. Specific policy solutions that were adopted in the context of a concrete historical moment can be imbued with strong normative feelings about how protection "ought" to be. This creates a status quo bias among the public that makes path-breaking reforms electorally dangerous.

Stage no. 2: Party competition[18]

Public preferences do not affect public policy directly but need to be introduced into the legislative arena by political parties. A large body of research has studied how parties compete for voters to maximize their own vote share and how, in this process, they also set the agenda for subsequent legislative activities. In the welfare state literature, by contrast, little attention has been given so far to this intermediate link between public preferences and policy. This section, therefore, outlines an argument about parties' electoral competition that is nested in the thesis.

When parties compete for votes, they often do so by emphasizing those issues that they believe will make them attractive to voters. This notion of *selective emphasis* is the basis of the issue competition literature (Robertson 1976; Budge et al. 1983). Often, there is an overlap between the issues parties focus on (Sigelmann & Buell 2004) due to exogenous events like natural disasters, or news reports on underperformance in the public sector that require all parties to focus on the same issue (Kingdon 1995: 94-100; Birkland 1998). If a party ignores a substantial, real-world problem, it is basically saying that it does not care about solving it. If a party's supporters find an issue unimportant, it may obviously be a good idea to ignore it even if other parties do not.

18   The section builds on *The Right and the Welfare State* (Jensen 2014) and *Electoral Competition and the Welfare State* (Green-Pedersen and Jensen 2019).

However, if the issue is salient to its supporters, this can have serious electoral consequences as they move to a more attentive alternative. Either way, (lack of) attention to issues is a potent way of signaling to voters what the party stands for (Robertson 1976; Budge et al. 1983; Green-Pedersen 2007).

Real-world problems that simultaneously affect a large group of voters infuse electoral competition with considerable dynamics, as those parties keen on signaling commitment scramble to make themselves heard. It consequently becomes important to understand both *the supply of problems* and *the distribution of demand for solutions* among voters and how these vary from one policy area to the next. The supply of problems tells us something about the underlying pressure for parties to pay attention to an area, while the distribution of demand for solutions indicates which parties want to signal a commitment to which areas.

Looking at various forms of life cycle and labor market risk protection, it is immediately obvious that the supply of problems is bound to be highly varied. This is due to the different expected outcomes and production processes with which they are associated. The expected outcomes range from ensuring good health over a secure old age to providing a livelihood for the jobless and other labor market outsiders, while the production processes range from running hospitals and elderly homes to paying cash benefits. The variety and nature of problems facing politicians across such diverse policy areas will be heterogeneous. According to the issue competition literature, this entails that the attention parties pay to them will be heterogeneous too.

Health care stands out from all other welfare state areas because of the technologically complicated production process. New treatments are constantly being invented and refined by the medical industry, which is one of the biggest and most innovative in the world. Costs are, as a result, under constant upward pressure (Newhouse 1992; Okunade & Murthy 2002; Chernew & Newhouse 2012). The never-ending stream of new and better treatments and the complicated organization of health care systems create a constant supply of news stories about underperformance, mistakes, and missed opportunities. In this way, the supply of problems in health care is very much a function of the modernization process, which is one of the main reasons why such a spectacularly innovative medical industry came about in the first place.

Public programs aimed exclusively at the old are different from health care (which, of course, treats many old people too) because the production process is normally much less complex. Paying out pensions is mostly a routine process, while organizing elderly care is more demanding. Still, the biggest source of problems in the area comes not from the inherent complexity of the production process, but from the inability to finance the area sufficiently. As the proportion of elderly people rises in many places, costs rise too. Moreover, as the modernization process has gradually increased people's standard of living, so have expectations about what a decent standard of living for the old entails. Returning to the elderly services of the 1950s would likely cause an outcry.

The core of labor market risk protection is a hodgepodge of unemployment protection, employment security, and active labor market and vocational training schemes. The supply of problems related to these policies stems mostly from sources other than the production process itself because the bulk of activities consists of paying and regulating cash benefits. Problems, instead, come from the inability of the government intervention to solve social problems like lack of incentives to accept jobs, the working poor, or a mismatch been demand and supply of skills. However, over time, the main driver of perceived problems is, arguably, the state of the economy. When the economy is booming, few expect parties to pay attention to labor market risk protection, while the reverse is true when the economy is down.

The distribution of demand for solutions follows from the discussions in Chapter 3 and the last section. All voters are keenly aware of the personal costs of life cycle risks, and those exposed are seen as deserving of public help. The implication is that all mainstream parties need to pay attention to life cycle risks to signal their commitment to the issues concerning their potential voters. Life cycle risks become *valence issues* because everybody agrees on their importance, leaving only the proper solutions to be debated (where there is more leeway for disagreement, as noted before). The exposure of labor market risks follows the socio-economic cleavages in society. The implication is that parties' attention will follow these cleavages too. Most importantly, parties of the left, such as the social democrats and socialists, will tend to focus more on labor market risk protection than the fiscal conservatives and other parties less interested in wooing those exposed to the vagaries of the labor market.

Stage no. 3: Public policy-making[19]

Parties' electoral competition is important not just because it creates a link between parties and voters, but also because it influences what policies the incoming government will pursue. Research shows that parties who win office tend to act on those issues that they emphasized before the election, presumably because not doing so can lead to an electoral backlash (Hofferbert & Budge 1992; Klingemann et al. 1994; Horn and Jensen 2017; Thomson et al. 2017). However, because of voters' inattention to the details of policy solutions, there is more than one way for parties to deliver to their constituency. This paves the way for considerable policy engineering, where elite actors try to maximize the gains of the special interests they represent. This section

19   This section draws on *Marketization via Compensation* (Jensen 2011), *Labor Market versus Life-course Risks* (Jensen 2012), *The Right and the Welfare State* (Jensen 2014), *Policy Instruments* (Jensen et al. 2018), and *Risky Business* (Lee et al. 2019).

explores the tension between electorally given constraints and elites' policy engineering.

The first thing to consider, however, is the relationship between the modernization process and the provision of life cycle risk protection. Life cycle risks have arguably always been social risks in the sense that they have been considered a collective responsibility. As far as we know, hunter-gatherer communities engaged in extensive resource-sharing to compensate the injured and frail (Kaplan et al. 2000; Sugiyama and Chacon 2000; Sugiyama 2004; Cosmides and Tooby 2005; Flannery and Marcus 2012); these are modes of communal risk protection that continued into recorded history (e.g., Porter 1997; Thane 2000). With the rise of the modern state and the resources of the modernization process, it became possible to shift the responsibility away from the family and local community and into the public realm. Still, the key distinction between communal and public risk protection is not the location of the risk pooling, but whether people have a legal entitlement to protection.[20] This is only the case for public risk protection.

Given the importance ascribed to life cycle risks by both voters and parties, one basic expectation is that the legal entitlements to life cycle risk protection will be introduced before legal entitlements to labor market risk protection. We know from historical accounts that the earliest welfare

---

20   This is also the gist of Marshall's (1992 [1950]: 8) concept of social rights.

programs in Europe were directed at life cycle risks. Bismarck's 1883 sickness insurance is traditionally considered the first modern welfare state legislation, followed by the 1884 accident insurance and the 1889 old age and disability insurance schemes. Germany's unemployment protection program was not introduced until 1927; that is, after a lag of around 40 years (Hicks, 1999: 51). How universal is this sequence? For the answer to this question, consult Figure 4.3, which displays the proportion of 183 of the world's countries that, in a given year, had adopted statutory legislation covering old age pensions, health care, and unemployment since 1900.

The proportion of countries with welfare programs increases with time, which is not surprising. What is interesting, though, is that the percentage of countries with old age pensions and health care is quite systematically about twice as large as the percentage of countries with an unemployment protection scheme. After 2005, the latest period of observation, the percentage for old age pensions is 99, for health care 91, and for unemployment protection 48. This is exactly what we would expect if countries prioritized life cycle risk over labor market risk protection.

Figure 4.3. Proportion of countries with statutory legislation

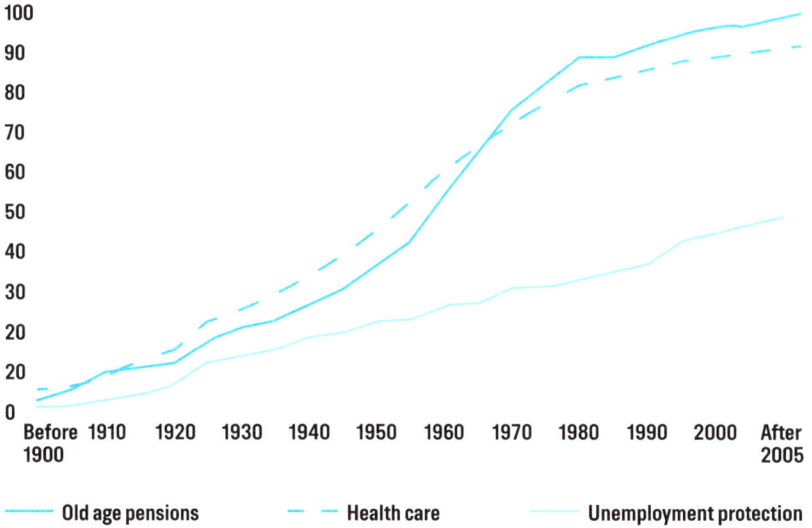

Source: International Labor Organization (ILO) (2015).

Note: 'Health care' is defined as programs providing help against disability, sickness, and injury.

The fact that a country has a social problem covered by national legislation may not necessarily entail that a large part of the citizenry is covered. The program may be for just a small group, for example civil servants or some other select occupation. It is therefore interesting to know the effective coverage rates to see if the pattern in Figure 4.3 reflects real differences. Figure 4.4 displays four measures of so-called effective coverage rates.[21] The horizontal axis reports effective coverage, ranging from 0 (no-one is covered) to 100 (everybody is covered). The vertical axis lists the number of countries.

Comparing the four measures, it is evident that effective coverage on average is much lower for unemployment than for old age pensions and health care. The comparably few countries with unemployment protection tend to have low coverage

21   The effective coverage rates are calculated by the International Labor Organization (2015) and refer to the year 2011, or the closest year available. Effective pension coverage is measured as the proportion of the population above statutory pensionable age receiving old age pensions. Effective unemployment protection coverage is measured as the proportion of unemployed receiving benefits. Effective health care coverage is measured in two ways, reflecting how an appropriate estimate is trickier to come up with for this area. One measure gives the proportion of the total population that has either health insurance or access to free health care. The second health coverage measure is composed of four variables and is more complex. The first is the percentage of the population not covered due to professional health staff deficit. The rationale for the measure is that a formal right to health care is irrelevant if there is not enough staff to provide the service in the first place. Methodologically, the challenge is to settle on the "needed" number of staff so that any deficit can be established. The International Labor Organization's measure solves this ingeniously. The measure is calculated in two steps. First, the ratio of health staff to the population is calculated for all countries. Second, the ratio of each individual country is compared to the median ratio among highly developed countries. The underlying assumption is that the median level among highly developed countries "guarantees at least basic [...] access to everybody" (International Labor Organization, 2010, 278). The second measure does the exact same thing as the first but compares the ratio of each country to an official World Health Organization benchmark. The third and fourth measures are the percentages of the population not covered due to financial deficit. They follow the same logic as the first two measures but rely on the proportion of health expenditure not paid for via out-of-pocket payments rather than the ratio of health staff. The difference between the two financial coverage gap measures is that the ratio is compared to two different benchmarks (for details, see International Labor Organization, 2015, 165-170). The four variables are collapsed into one, capturing the degree of coverage deficit for the sick (Cronbach's α = .94).

rates. Some countries also have low coverage rates for old age pensions and health care, but the average coverage rate is much higher than for unemployment. Across all countries, 53 percent have pension coverage, and 61 percent are covered by a health care scheme. This compares favorably with the 32 percent of all jobless who on average have access to unemployment protection. If we allow for the fact that many countries have no unemployment protection scheme at all, average coverage drops to a measly 12 percent.

It is noteworthy that health care coverage is somewhat better than old age pension coverage. Many countries have close to universal coverage, as seen in the bottom-left graph. The alternative health care coverage measure displayed in the bottom-right graph cannot be compared directly with the other three because it does not measure a proportion of the relevant citizenry but rather the so-called coverage gap, that is, how adequate health care provision is. A higher value indicates higher quality. It is clear that high coverage is matched by high adequacy.

Figure 4.4. Number of countries and effective coverage

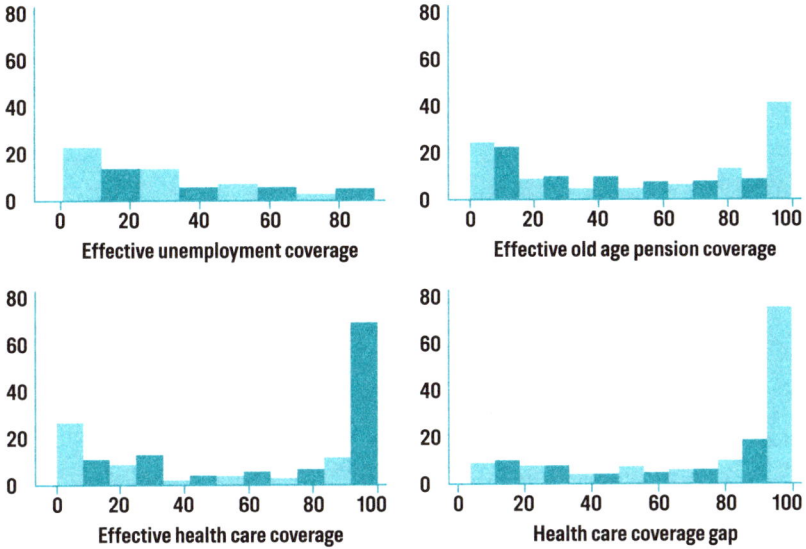

Effective unemployment coverage

Effective old age pension coverage

Effective health care coverage

Health care coverage gap

Source: International Labor Organization (2015).

The essence of my argument is that life cycle risk protection will be prioritized as countries grow affluent, as part of the modernization process. Figure 4.5 displays correlations between the effective coverage rates used in Figure 4.4 (now shown on the vertical axis) and GDP per capita measured as purchasing power-parities-adjusted US dollars (on the horizontal axis). GDP is the standard measure in the literature for capturing the degree of modernization. The pattern is striking. Old age pension and health care coverage are strongly correlated with GDP per capita. For countries with a GDP per capita of roughly around 10,000 USD, coverage is 50 percent for old age pension, 56 percent for health care, but only 5 percent for unemployment protection. When GDP per capita reaches 19,000-21,000 USD, coverage is 75, 97, and 39 percent, respectively.

Figure 4.5. Effective coverage and GDP per capita

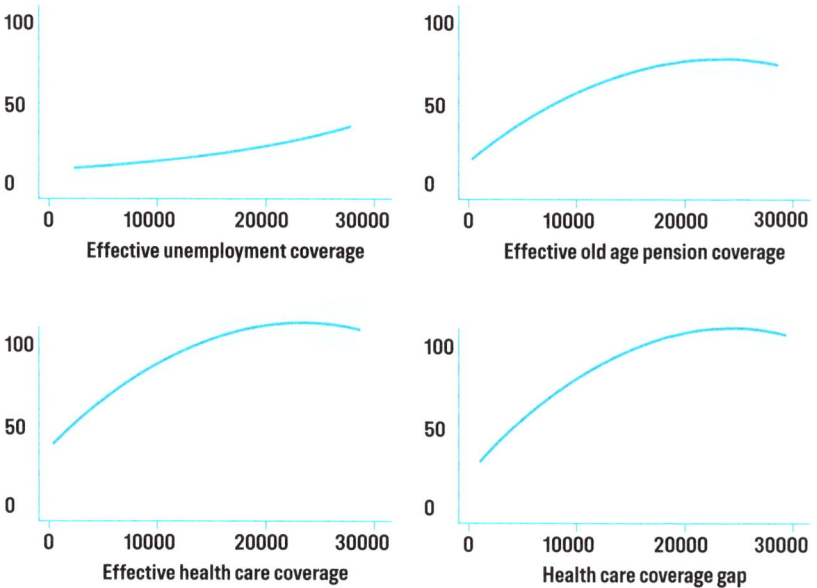

Source: International Labor Organization (2015).

It is once again noteworthy that health care coverage is even more sensitive to rising GDP than old age pension coverage. First, the proportion of the population covered by a health care scheme increases faster than the proportion covered by an old age pension. Moreover, if we look at the health care coverage gap, we see that minimally adequate health care is provided at rather low levels of affluence. When GDP per capita approaches 10,000 USD, the coverage gap is at 90.[22]

Figures 4.3, 4.4, and 4.5 indicate just how much more important life cycle risk protection appears to be compared to labor market risk protection. The underlying assumption is that the former type of risk enjoys bipartisan support because all major voter groups demand protection against it. In the context of the welfare state literature, which focuses on countries that are comparably wealthy, this makes the actions of center-right governments particularly interesting. Apart from the fact that the literature has been preoccupied with the social democrats and other left-wing parties, the center-right is important to study because they usually are assumed to harbor strong anti-welfare state sentiments. However, it follows from my argument that this is too simple a characterization. Rather, the center-right will simultaneously ensure adequate life cycle risk protection that covers a large segment of the population and try to do so in a way that benefits its core constituency most.

First, empirically, there are no statistically significant differences between the investments in life cycle risk protection by center-left and center-right

22   Figure 4.5 displays the bivariate correlation between GDP per capita and the effect of coverage measures. The conclusion from the figure remains when controlling for democracy levels and socio-economic pressure in the form of the unemployment rate and proportion of people aged 65 or more in a country.

governments in Western democracies. There are, by contrast and to this day, substantial partisan differences in the domain of labor market risk protection, where the center-left is more generous than the center-right in terms of both spending and the actual entitlements of claimants (Jensen 2012; 2014; Zohlenhöfer et al. 2013). The British experience may be particularly instructive because governments there are normally made up of a single party with an absolute majority in Parliament. This entails that the Conservatives, when in government, are free to act as they want—with the main constraint being the need for re-election and, hence, the preferences of the voters. The Thatcher, Major, and Cameron cabinets introduced big cutbacks to the labor market protection system, essentially reducing its generosity to pre-war levels. In the domain of old age pensions and health care, the Conservatives adopted a wildly different approach, with frequent expansions of both entitlements and public spending (for an overview, see Jensen 2014; Jensen et al. 2018).

Importantly, the fact that the center-right refrains from outright cutbacks does not imply that all governments act alike. Partisan differences emerge in the domain of life cycle risks when moving from *how much* money is being spent to *how* the money is spent. Center-right governments stand out for their preference for so-called *marketization via layering*. The purpose is to introduce private insurance elements that typically benefit the center-right's constituency but do so by adding tax deductions and rebates on top of the existing system. In this way, center-right governments can signal a true commitment to maintaining life cycle risk protection while, at the same time, catering to their own narrower voter base (for analyses of this strategy, see Jensen 2011; 2014).

It is a crucial point of my argument that center-right parties and, by extension, their supporters, are not *a priori* committed to public solutions (recall again: people do not have strong intuitions about solutions, only risks). If public solutions become dominant in a country, voters will normally end up feeling comfortable with these and eventually develop a strong status quo bias. However, in the context of no preexisting public solutions, the supporters of center-right parties have no such affinities. In this scenario, center-right parties must provide life cycle risk protection, but the exact mode of delivery is much less relevant. This means that countries with a dominant center-right can maintain privately organized, though almost always publicly subsidized, life cycle risk protection, as long as this ensures effective risk protection for an electoral majority. Conversely, in the event the center-left gains power and pushes through a public solution instead, it can be electorally dangerous for the center-right to revert to the old private solution.[23] This is why, over time, all Western democracies have

---

23   Note that the center-left can face stiff opposition too when trying to introduce public solutions, as recently seen with Obamacare. However, the American experience nonetheless still illustrates how government, even in the most welfare-skeptical Western nation, has over the course of the past century gradually taken over more and more responsibility.

crawled toward public provision as the default. In the formulation of Huber and Stephens (2001: 28), this is a so-called ratchet effect—a one-way street where policies either remain stable or move in a single direction: The center-right can stick to their favorite private solutions, that especially benefit their core constituency, as long as they hold on to power. However, once a country goes public, it rarely returns.

In today's world of mostly publicly provided life cycle risk protection, the enduring popularity of these schemes makes outright retrenchment an electorally high-risk game for politicians of all partisan hues. Sometimes, of course, governments cannot avoid retrenching life cycle risk protection, but it comes with a steep electoral price. In a recent article with three colleagues on the electoral consequences of retrenchment in Britain and Denmark, I conclude that voters punish cutbacks in pensions considerably more than cutbacks in unemployment protection (Lee et al. 2019).

One may speculate that this popularity makes governments particularly cautious when implementing cutbacks in life cycle risk protection as opposed to labor market risk protection. Pierson (1994) argues that one way to avoid getting blamed for unpopular decisions is to employ obfuscation strategies where the causal chain between the decision-making politicians and the negative effects on people's risk protection is blurred. One important way of doing this is by using very technical policy instruments that are "invisible" to most voters.

These may include changing indexation rules or the wage sum upon which benefits are calculated. Here, too, new empirical evidence suggests that there is a marked difference between life cycle and labor market risk protection: Cutbacks in old age pensions are much more likely to come in the guise of "invisible" policy instruments, compared to cutbacks in unemployment protection (for an analysis of these patterns, see Jensen et al. 2018).

Conclusion

This chapter has argued that the politics of life cycle risks is distinct from the politics of labor market risks. The distinctiveness is apparent at the level of public preferences, parties' electoral competition, and public policy-making. Life cycle risk protection is much more universally popular than protection against labor market risks, which forces all mainstream parties to pay attention to these issues and the social problems associated with them when they fight over votes. In combination, voters' expectations and parties' commitments mean that life cycle risk protection tends to be prioritized over labor market risk protection—both historically across the globe and today in Western democracies. That said, my argument should not be read as a disqualification of the role of political elites. Elites are vital actors, but their room for maneuver is smaller in the domain of life cycle risks than in the domain of labor market risks. Still, with the usage of clever strategies, it is possible here, too, to make policies that benefit some groups more than others.

Chapter 5
Inequality and the bifurcation of the welfare state

One of the most important changes in Western societies over the past couple of decades has been the rising levels of socio-economic inequalities (OECD 2011; Piketty 2014; Jensen and van Kersbergen 2017: 55-61). The Anglo-Saxon countries in particular have witnessed higher inequality, but the trend is visible everywhere. More extensive differences in health outcomes and social mobility have come with economic inequality, thereby intensifying already vicious feedback between people's family backgrounds, work histories, and lifestyle choices. To some observers, this new reality of more and more unequal societies is the key challenge facing welfare states today.

The standard explanation in the welfare state literature for these trends relates to the rise of the post-industrial economy and the associated erosion of the political clout of those individuals exposed to labor market risks (for a review, see Jensen and van Kersbergen 2017: 77-94, 133-165). The rising number of low-paid service jobs and the simultaneous decline of the industrial sector have eroded unions' membership base and weakened their ability to keep wage levels compressed and fight the retrenchment of labor market risk protection. Economic globalization, which has today reached unprecedented heights and intensity, forces governments to reduce taxes, and consequently welfare state spending, to stay attractive to footloose capital. Immigration and the rise of value-based politics have, finally, shifted the political landscape to the right and led to the introduction of welfare chauvinist policies.

All these explanations are highly plausible, but probably also only partial, since they overlook the politics of life cycle risks. I argue that another source of rising inequalities lies in the fact that life cycle risk protection (which is enjoyed by everybody and, hence, not very redistributive) is slowly crowding out the more redistributive labor market risk protection (which is often targeted at the poor and labor market outsiders). The root cause of the crowding out is the combination of widespread popular demand and rising problem pressure in the domain of life cycle risks. As I explained previously, what is considered adequate protection against life cycle risks is constantly changing, and rarely toward cheaper options. Health care is particularly prominent in this regard. New treatments are constantly being invented, putting unrelenting upward pressure on costs. Denying voters access to the best available treatments can be electorally dangerous for politicians seeking reelection.

The crowding out is visible at the level of both parties' electoral competition and public policy-making. Since the 1980s, parties' levels of attention to health care has roughly doubled, whereas attention to labor market risk protection has either remained stable or decreased (Green-Pedersen and Jensen 2019). Public spending on health care and old age pensions has seen similar hikes. Across the Organisation for Economic Cooperation and Development (OECD), public spending on old age pension as a percentage of the GDP has gone from 5.1 percent in 1980 to 7.7 percent in 2013, while health care spending has increased from 4.2 to 6 percent during the same period (OECD 2017). These increases are the product of augmenting problem pressures (more old people, better treatments), but there is nothing automatic, or predestined, about them. Problem pressures are allowed to spill over into more spending because of voters' expectations. If it were not for these, it would be easy for governments to keep spending at bay. It is the combination of a unique supply of problems and demand for solutions that makes life cycle risk protection a special political issue that requires reelection-motivated politicians to keep pouring in money. Not that it seems to matter much to the voters, however. According to the International Social Survey Programme's Role of Government IV, 68.5 and 80 percent of the public in Western democracies want more or much more spending on old age pensions and health care, respectively.[24]

It is in the context of this seemingly insatiable appetite for life cycle risk protection that politicians are operating. It adds an important factor to the laundry list of reasons for governments to curtail labor market risk protection. By cutting the latter, which is much less universally popular, budget space is freed that can be prioritized for life cycle risk protection. It has been documented many times that the entitlements related to the labor market have been reformed extensively. Employment security has been lowered, and unemployment protection made less generous (Korpi and Palme 2003; Allan and Scruggs 2004; Clasen and Clegg 2007; Jensen 2014). That the cutbacks can be justified with reference to the necessities of post-industrial and highly globalized economies only makes the reallocation easier. The result has been an expanding gap between life cycle and labor market risk protection. The former, aimed at the large electoral majorities of the public, is made ever more generous and the latter ever more meager. Effectively, this heightens the exposure of marginalized groups and inadvertently

---

24 Incidentially, this also constitutes a critique of Wlezien's well-known thermostat model of public preferences (Wlezien 1995). Contrary to this model's prediction, public preferences for life cycle risk protection do not appear to be influenced by additional spending.

fosters inequality, as the incomes of the poor and labor market outsiders are squeezed.[25]

The argument outlined here flies in the face of received wisdom in the welfare state literature. In a widely cited article, Korpi and Palme (1998) propose that the key to highly redistributive welfare states is to forge an alliance between the middle class and the workers by having everybody join the same programs. When the middle class gets a share of the cake, they will push the government for more generosity, and because the workers are part of it too, they benefit as well. This is why middle-class-oriented welfare states tend to create more redistribution even though benefits are not going exclusively to the poor. As Korpi and Palme formalize it, redistribution is a combined function of a welfare state's redistributive profile and the size of its budget. Welfare states that include the middle class simply have such big budgets that they end up redistributing more than the small budgets of targeted welfare states.

The best example of middle-class programs is health care, which almost everywhere in the developed world includes all citizens, followed by old age pensions, which are typically also available (though not always equally generous) for most people. Incidentally, these are also the programs providing life cycle risk protection. In my narrative, however, these programs are not the source of equality,

---

25   Pontusson and Weisstanner (2018) present an argument that supplements mine. They argue that the increasing concentration of labor market risks among the poor and less educated decreases the willingness of middle-class citizens to sponsor generous labor market risk protection.

rather the opposite. My reasoning is that Korpi and Palme overlook the fact that even when a country has generous life cycle risk protection programs like health care, the poor and labor market outsiders still depend on the income maintenance of labor market risk protection. They also overlook that the size of the budget is not indefinite and that popular demand for life cycle protection is virtually limitless. Just because the middle class is on board does not mean that spending on everybody can go up.

Figure 5.1 provides an illustration of this point. It presents the average tax revenue as a percent of the GDP across the OECD from 1965 to 2015. The blue line represents the 10-year averages, while the blue dashed line represents the yearly averages. The trend is striking. In the first three decades, spending rose constantly, but at ever smaller increments. For the past 20 years, expansion has halted and even retracted. Taxation has clearly reached a ceiling. What Korpi and Palme (1998) seem to forget is that big welfare states are overwhelmingly paid for by the income and indirect taxes of the middle class (Beramendi and Cusack 2006; Beramendi and Rueda 2007). In other words, the middle class may like a big, encompassing welfare state, but they are paying for it. This creates a trade-off between wanting both generous welfare and reasonably low taxes. As Giger and Nelson (2013) have shown, quite a large portion of citizens are so-called conditional welfare believers, meaning that they simultaneously cherish both low taxes and generous welfare. Given this, it is no wonder that politicians have been willing and able to halt the growth of government.

Figure 5.1. Tax revenue as a percentage of GDP in the OECD

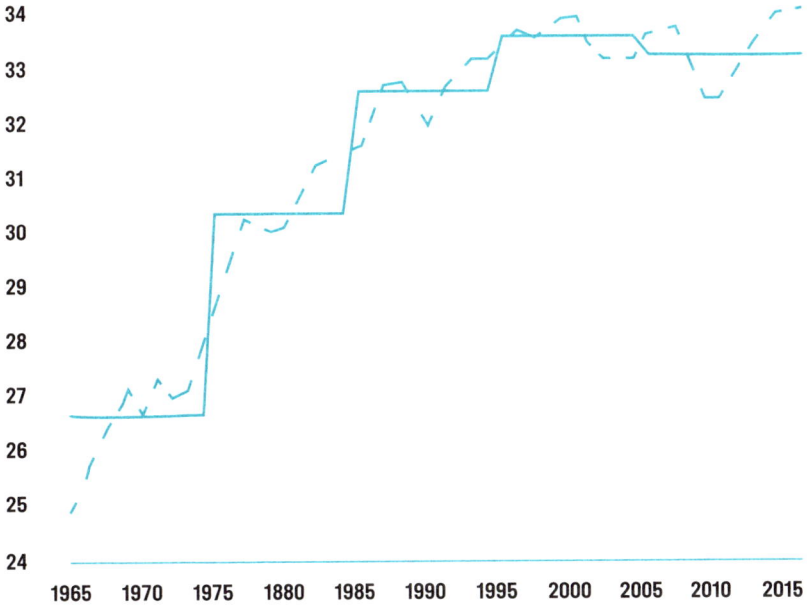

Source: OECD (2017).

No matter the cause of the ceiling effect, the takeaway is simple but crucial: The size of the government cannot meaningfully be regarded as a variable that can increase so that everybody—the poor and the middle class alike—can have their share. Instead, what has happened is that the generosity of labor market risk protection has been lowered in part to pay for continuing expansion of life cycle protection.

While the poor and labor market outsiders can enjoy these too, they are still hurt when the programs dedicated more exclusively to them are slashed.[26]

Given the logic of the argument I have tried to present above, there is nothing indicating that this bifurcation of the welfare state is likely to stop anytime soon. People's expectations about life cycle risk protection are unlikely to become less demanding. If anything, expectations will continue to become ever costlier to meet. However, for reelection-oriented politicians, systematically saying no to rising demands will be close to impossible. Cutbacks to life cycle risk protection may occur in the future, of course, but they will be the exceptions that prove the rule that life cycle risk protection will steadily crowd out labor market risk protection. The result will be a bifurcated welfare state where one set of programs will be generously funded while the other, the one aimed at the poor and labor market outsiders, will become increasingly stingy.

26 Isolating the effect of labor market risk protection reforms is difficult. In a recent report for the Danish Economic Council, Kjeldsen (2016) uses high-quality register-based data from Denmark to decompose the sources of the rising level of inequality. She finds that the dramatic drop in the number of people claiming unemployment insurance since the 1990s is a substantial source of inequality (a drop that, in turn, is due to a series of labor market reforms in combination with an improved economy).

—

In Chapter 1, I explained that the core claim of this thesis is that the fundamental differences in the nature of life cycle and labor market risks create distinct political dynamics across the two domains. This is why we ought to talk of a dual risk model of the politics of the welfare state. The differences are visible at all stages of the political process from the public's beliefs and preferences to the parties' electoral competition and, finally, public policy-making. I believe that by focusing on the politics of life cycle risks we gain analytical leverage over a set of issues that have been either ignored or ill-explained by the existing literature: Why are some welfare programs much more popular than others? Under what conditions will fiscal conservatives adopt a pro-welfare position? Why are some welfare programs characterized by a constant rise in public spending while others have seen retrenchment?

By way of conclusion, let me emphasize that the argument presented here is meant to supplement, not replace, the conventional narrative of the welfare state's development. As I went to some length explaining in Chapter 2, the combined effort of welfare state scholars during the past decades has created what I would argue is a standard account of the welfare state's development. Disagreement about the details is legion, but seen from the outside, a common core is clearly evident. Although sometimes overlooked, the modernization process constitutes the analytical center of the literature. It is the source of labor market risks and the generator of political conflict. By now, we thus have a solid, though admittedly not perfect, understanding both of citizens' perception of labor market risks and of the resulting politics.

My argument also highlights the important role of the modernization process, but underscores that its effects will vary dramatically across the two risk domains. First, effective protection against life cycle risks requires monetary and technological resources that did not exist prior to the industrial revolution. Communal protection—the family and local community—has always been there, but from the point of view of the welfare state, the modernization process is the trigger. It is trivial that no country had a proper welfare state before the 20th century because the means to provide it did not exist, but it is far from trivial that the first risks to be catered to when the opportunity arrived were almost invariantly those of the life cycle.

Second, the modernization process has had a deep and persistent effect on the political structure of all developed democracies. The industrial revolution sparked the labor movement and the associated conflict between capital and labor, which, in turn, became institutionalized in the party system and the welfare state. The rigidity of both is one of the main reasons why the emergence of the post-industrial economy has meant hardship for many. However, these "frozen landscapes" not only condition how well countries can handle new labor market risks but also how the politics of life cycle risks play out. There are no cleavages separating the sick from the healthy and the old from the young, and, hence, no parties mobilizing these groups. In a nutshell, most party systems are organized around conflicts about the labor market, not the life cycle. This forms the impetus for the special partisan politics of life cycle risks, with—not least—fiscally conservative parties having to handle multiple and often contradictory goals at the same time.

Third, as the modernization process keeps un-folding, demands for more spending on life cycle risk protection become louder. Since the level of taxation has reached a ceiling, this leads to a gradual crowd-ing out of labor market risk protection as money is shifted to life cycle programs, with potentially big knock-on effects on socio-economic inequalities. If for no other reason, then, this crowding out is a sig-nal to conventional scholars of the welfare state that they ought to pay more attention to the politics of life cycle risks.

References

Allan, J. P., & Scruggs, L. (2004). Political partisanship and welfare state reform in advanced industrial societies. *American Journal of Political Science, 48*(3), 496-512.

Alt, J., & Iversen, T. (2017). Inequality, labor market segmentation, and preferences for redistribution. *American Journal of Political Science, 61*(1), 21-36.

Arndt., C. & Jensen, C. (2017). Partivalg og holdninger til velfærdsstaten. In K. M. Hansen and R. Stubager (eds.), *Oprør fra udkanten: Folketingsvalget 2015*. Copenhagen: Djøf/Jurist- og Økonomforbundet, 245-263.

Baldwin, P. (1990). *The Politics of Social Solidarity*. Cambridge University Press.

Barber IV, B., Beramendi, P., & Wibbels, E. (2013). The behavioral foundations of social politics: Evidence from surveys and a laboratory democracy. *Comparative Political Studies, 46*(10), 1155-1189.

Bartels, L. M. (2005). Homer gets a tax cut: Inequality and public policy in the American mind. *Perspectives on Politics, 3*(1), 15-31.

Baumgartner, F. R., & Jones, B. D. (1993). *Agendas and Instability in American Politics*. University of Chicago Press.

Béland, Daniel, & Cox, Robert H. (2011). *Ideas and Politics in Social Science Research*. New York: Oxford University Press.

Beramendi, P., Häusermann, S., Kitschelt, H., & Kriesi, H. (2015). *The Politics of Advanced Capitalism*. Cambridge University Press.

Beramendi, P., & Rueda, D. (2007). Social democracy constrained: indirect taxation in industrialized democracies. *British Journal of Political Science, 37*(4), 619-641.

Birkland, T. A. (1998). Focusing events, mobilization, and agenda setting. *Journal of Public Policy, 18*(1), 53-74.

Blank, R., & Burau, V. (2010). Comparative Health Policy. Third Edition. Palgrave.

Blendon, R. (2011). *American Public Opinion and Health Care.* SAGE.

Blyth, M. (2002). *Great Transformations: Economic Ideas and Institutional Change in the Twentieth Century.* Cambridge University Press.

Boix, C. (1999). Setting the rules of the game: the choice of electoral systems in advanced democracies. *American Political Science Review, 93*(3), 609-624.

Boix, C. (2010). Electoral markets, party strategies, and proportional representation. *American Political Science Review, 104*(2), 404-413.

Bonoli, G. (2007). Time matters: Postindustrialization, new social risks, and welfare state adaptation in advanced industrial democracies. *Comparative Political Studies, 40*(5), 495-520.

Boyd, K. M. (2000). Disease, illness, sickness, health, healing and wholeness: exploring some elusive concepts. *Medical Humanities, 26*(1), 9-17.

Brooks, C., & Manza, J. (2007). *Why Welfare States Persist: Public Opinion and the Future of Social Provision.* Chicago: University of Chicago Press.

Budge, I., & Farlie, D. (1983). Party competition—Selective emphasis or direct confrontation? An alternative view with data. In H. Daalder & P. Mair (eds.), *West European Party systems, Continuity & change* (pp. 267-305). London: Sage Publications.

Carpini, M. X. D., & Keeter, S. (1996). *What Americans know about politics and why it matters.* New Haven: Yale University Press.

Chernew, M. E., & Newhouse, J. P. (2012). Health care spending growth. In *Handbook of health economics* (Vol. 2, pp. 1-43). Elsevier.

Clasen, J., & Clegg, D. (2007). Levels and levers of conditionality: Measuring change within welfare states. In J. Clasen & N. Siegel (eds.), *Investigating Welfare State Change: The 'Dependent Variable Problem' in Comparative Analysis* (pp. 166-197). Cheltenham: Edward Elgar.

Cosmides, L., & Tooby, J. (2005). Neurocognitive adaptations designed for social exchange. In D. Buss (ed.), *The handbook of evolutionary psychology.* Wiley.

Cusack, T. R., & Beramendi, P. (2006). Taxing work. *European Journal of Political Research, 45*(1), 43-73.

Cusack, T. R., Iversen, T., & Soskice, D. (2007). Economic interests and the origins of electoral systems. *American Political Science Review, 101*(3), 373-391.

Cusack, T., Iversen, T., & Soskice, D. (2010). Coevolution of capitalism and political representation: The choice of electoral systems. *American Political Science Review, 104*(2), 393-403.

Cutright, P. (1965). Political structure, economic development, and national social security programs. *American Journal of Sociology, 70*(5), 537-550.

Donaldson, M. S. (2014). Nutrition and cancer: A review of the evidence for an anti-cancer diet. *Nutrition Journal, 3*(1), 19.

Dugan, A., & Wendt, N. (2014). *Families struggling to afford food in OECD countries.* Gallup News. Downloaded at: http://news.gallup.com/poll/170795/families-struggling-afford-food-oecd-countries.aspx. Accessed on December 11, 2017.

Elo, I. T. (2009). Social class differentials in health and mortality: Patterns and explanations in comparative perspective. *Annual Review of Sociology, 35*, 553-572.

Emmenegger, P. (2014). *The power to dismiss.* New York and Oxford: Oxford University Press.

Emmenegger, P., Häusermann, S., Palier, B., & Seeleib-Kaiser, M. (2012). *The age of dualization: The changing face of inequality in deindustrializing societies.* New York and Oxford: Oxford University Press.

Evans, J. S. B. (2008). Dual-processing accounts of reasoning, judgment, and social cognition. *Annual Review Psychology, 59*, 255-278.

Evans, J. S. B., & Stanovich, K. E. (2013). Dual-process theories of higher cognition: Advancing the debate. *Perspectives on Psychological Science, 8*(3), 223-241.

Flannery, K., & Marcus, J. (2012). *The creation of inequality.* Harvard University Press.

Giger, N., & Nelson, M. (2012). The welfare state or the economy? Preferences, constituencies, and strategies for retrenchment. *European Sociological Review, 29*(5), 1083-1094.

Gingrich, J., & Ansell, B. (2012). Preferences in context: Micro preferences, macro contexts, and the demand for social policy. *Comparative Political Studies, 45*(12), 1624-1654.

Green-Pedersen, C. (2007). The growing importance of issue competition: The changing nature of party competition in Western Europe. *Political Studies, 55*(3), 607-628.

Green-Pedersen, C. & Jensen, C. (2019). Electoral Competition and the Welfare State. *West European Politics, 42*(4), 803-822.

Hacker, J. S. (2002). *The divided welfare state: The battle over public and private social benefits in the United States.* Cambridge University Press.

Hacker, J. S., & Pierson, P. (2010). *Winner-take-all politics: How Washington made the rich richer—and turned its back on the middle class.* New York: Simon and Schuster.

Hall, P. A. (1993). Policy paradigms, social learning, and the state: the case of economic policymaking in Britain. *Comparative Politics,* 25(3), 275-296.

Häusermann, S., Kurer, T., & Schwander, H. (2016). Sharing the risk? Households, labor market vulnerability and social policy preferences in Western Europe. *Journal of Politics, 78*(4), 1045-60.

Hicks, A. M. (1999). *Social democracy and welfare capitalism: A century of income security politics.* Cornell University Press.

Horn, A., & Jensen, C. (2017). When and why politicians do not keep their welfare promises. *European Journal of Political Research, 56*(2), 381-400.

Huber, E., Ragin, C., & Stephens, J. D. (1993). Social democracy, Christian democracy, constitutional structure, and the welfare state. *American Journal of Sociology, 99*(3), 711-749.

Huckfeldt, R., & Sprague, J. (1987). Networks in context: The social flow of political information. *American Political Science Review, 81*(4), 1197-1216.

Huckfeldt, R., Plutzer, E., & Sprague, J. (1993). Alternative contexts of political behavior: Churches, neighborhoods, and individuals. *The Journal of Politics, 55*(2), 365-381.

Immergut, E. M. (1990). Institutions, veto points, and policy results: A comparative analysis of health care. *Journal of Public Policy, 10*(4), 391-416.

Immergut, E. M., Anderson, K. M., & Schulze, I. (2007). *The handbook of West European pension politics.* Oxford University Press.

International Labor Organization (2010). *Social Security Report 2010/11.* Geneva: ILO.

International Labor Organization (2015). *Social Security Report 2014/15.* Geneva: ILO.

Iversen, T., & Rosenbluth, F. M. (2010). *Women, work, and politics: The political economy of gender inequality.* Yale University Press.

Iversen, T., & Soskice, D. (2001). An asset theory of social policy preferences. *American Political Science Review, 95*(4), 875-893.

Iversen, T., & Soskice, D. (2006). Electoral institutions and the politics of coalitions: Why some democracies redistribute more than others. *American Political Science Review, 100*(2), 165-181.

Iversen, T., & Soskice, D. (2009). Distribution and redistribution: The shadow of the nineteenth century. *World Politics, 61*(3), 438-486.

Iversen, T., & Soskice, D. (2015). Democratic limits to redistribution: Inclusionary versus exclusionary coalitions in the knowledge economy. *World Politics, 67*(2), 185-225.

Iversen, T., & Wren, A. (1998). Equality, employment, and budgetary restraint: the trilemma of the service economy. *World Politics, 50*(4), 507-546.

Jensen, C. (2011). Marketization via compensation: Health care and the politics of the right in advanced industrialized nations. *British Journal of Political Science, 41*(4), 907-926.

Jensen, C. (2012). Labour market- versus life course-related social policies: understanding cross-programme differences. *Journal of European Public Policy, 19*(2), 275-291.

Jensen, C. (2014). *The Right and the Welfare State.* New York and Oxford: Oxford University Press.

Jensen, C., & Petersen, M. B. (2017). The deservingness heuristic and the politics of health care. *American Journal of Political Science, 61*(1), 68-83.

Jensen, C. & van Kersbergen, K. (2017). *The Politics of Inequality.* Palgrave.

Jensen, C., Arendt, C., Lee, S. & Wenzelburger, G. (2018). Policy instruments and welfare state reform. *Journal of European Social Policy, 28*(2), 161-176.

Jones, B. D. (2001). *Politics and the architecture of choice: Bounded rationality and governance.* University of Chicago Press.

Jones, B. D., & Baumgartner, F. R. (2005). *The politics of attention: How government prioritizes problems.* University of Chicago Press.

Kahneman, D., & Frederick, S. (2002). Representativeness revisited: Attribute substitution in intuitive judgment. In T. Gilovich, D. Griffin, & D. Kahneman (eds.), *Heuristics and Biases: The Psychology of Intuitive Judgment.* Cambridge University Press.

Kaplan, H., Hill, K., Lancaster, J., & Hurtado, M. A. (2000). A theory of human life history evolution: Diet, intelligence, and longevity. *Evolutionary Anthropology Issues News and Reviews, 9*(4), 156-185.

Katzenstein, P. J. (1985). *Small states in world markets: Industrial policy in Europe.* Cornell University Press.

Kingdon, J. W. (1995). *Agendas, alternatives, and public policies.* New York: HarperCollins.

Kitschelt, H., & Rehm, P. (2014). Occupations as a site of political preference formation. *Comparative Political Studies, 47*(12), 1670-1706.

Kjeldsen, M. M. (2016). *Dekomponering af Den Stigende Gini-koefficient.* Copenhagen: The Danish Economic Council.

Korpi, W. (1983). *The Democratic Class Struggle.* London: Routledge.

Korpi, W. (1989). Power, politics, and state autonomy in the development of social citizenship: Social rights during sickness in eighteen OECD countries since 1930. *American Sociological Review, 54*(3), 309-328.

Korpi, W. (2006). Power resources and employer-centered approaches in explanations of welfare states and varieties of capitalism: Protagonists, consenters, and antagonists. *World Politics, 58*(2), 167-206.

Korpi, W., & Palme, J. (1998). The paradox of redistribution and strategies of equality: Welfare state institutions, inequality, and poverty in the Western countries. *American Sociological Review, 63*(5), 661-687.

Korpi, W., & Palme, J. (2003). New politics and class politics in the context of austerity and globalization: Welfare state regress in 18 countries, 1975-95. *American Political Science Review, 97*(3), 425-446.

Kunda, Z. (1990). The case for motivated reasoning. *Psychological bulletin, 108*(3), 480-496.

Lee, S., Jensen, C., Arndt, C., & Wenzelburger, G. (2019). Risky business? Welfare state reforms and government support in Britain and Denmark. *British Journal of Political Science*. Early view.

Leeper, T. J., & Slothuus, R. (2014). Political parties, motivated reasoning, and public opinion formation. *Political Psychology, 35*(S1), 129-156.

Lewis, J. (1992). Gender and the development of welfare regimes. *Journal of European Social Policy, 2*(3), 159-173.

Loewenstein, G. F., Weber, E. U., Hsee, C. K., & Welch, N. (2001). Risk as feelings. *Psychological Bulletin, 127*(2), 267-286.

Mackenbach, J. P., Stirbu, I., Roskam, A. J. R., Schaap M. M., Menvielle, G., Leinsalu, M., & Kunst, A. E. (2008). Socioeconomic inequalities in health in 22 European countries. *New England Journal of Medicine, 358*(23), 2468-2481.

March, J. G., & Olsen, J. P. (2010). *Rediscovering Institutions*. Simon and Schuster.

Mares, I. (2003). *The politics of social risk: Business and welfare state development*. Cambridge University Press.

Marmot, M. (2005). Social determinants of health inequalities. *The Lancet, 365*(9464), 1099-1104.

Marshall, T. H. (1992 [1950]). *Citizenship and social class*. Pluto Press.

Maslow, A. H. (1943). A theory of human motivation. *Psychological Review, 50*(4), 370-396.

Meara, E. R., Richards, S., & Cutler, D. M. (2008). The gap gets bigger: changes in mortality and life expectancy, by education, 1981-2000. *Health Affairs, 27*(2), 350-360.

Meltzer, A. H., & Richard, S. F. (1981). A rational theory of the size of government. *The Journal of Political Economy, 89*(5), 914-927.

Mettler, S. (2011). *The submerged state: How invisible government policies undermine American democracy*. University of Chicago Press.

Moene, K. O., & Wallerstein, M. (2001). Inequality, social insurance, and redistribution. *American Political Science Review, 95*(4), 859-874.

Morgan, K. J. (2013). Path shifting of the welfare state: Electoral competition and the expansion of work-family policies in Western Europe. *World Politics, 65*(1), 73-115.

Mosimann, N., & Pontusson, J. (2017). Solidaristic unionism and support for redistribution in contemporary Europe. *World Politics, 69*(3), 448-492.

Newhouse, J. P. (1992). Medical care costs: How much welfare loss? *The Journal of Economic Perspectives, 6*(3), 3-21.

Nguyen, D., Petersen, M. B., & Koch, A. (2017). *Upper-body strength and conflict resolution in human males.* Working paper.

OECD (2011). *Divided we stand: Why inequality keeps rising.* Paris: OECD Publishing.

OECD (2017). OECD.Stat. Accessed at http://stats.oecd.org/

Okunade, A. A., & Murthy, V. N. (2002). Technology as a 'major driver' of health care costs: A cointegration analysis of the Newhouse conjecture. *Journal of Health Economics, 21*(1), 147-159.

Orloff, A. S. (1993). Gender and the social rights of citizenship: The comparative analysis of gender relations and welfare states. *American Sociological Review, 58*(3), 303-328.

Palier, B. (ed.) (2010). *A long goodbye to Bismarck? The politics of welfare reforms in continental Europe.* Amsterdam: Amsterdam University Press.

Petersen, M. B. (2012). Social welfare as small-scale help: Evolutionary psychology and the deservingness heuristic. *American Journal of Political Science, 56*(1), 1-16.

Petersen, M. B., Slothuus, R., Stubager, R., & Togeby, L. (2011). Deservingness versus values in public opinion on welfare: The automaticity of the deservingness heuristic. *European Journal of Political Research, 50*(1), 24-52.

Petersen, M. B., Sznycer, D., Cosmides, L., & Tooby, J. (2012). Who deserves help? Evolutionary psychology, social emotions, and public opinion about welfare. *Political Psychology, 33*(3), 395-418.

Pierson, P. (1994). *Dismantling the welfare state? Reagan, Thatcher, and the politics of retrenchment.* Cambridge: Cambridge University Press.

Piketty, T. (2014). *Capital in the 21st century.* Cambridge: Harvard University Press.

Polyani, K. (2001 [1944]). *The great transformation.* Boston: Beacon Press.

Pontusson, J., & Weisstanner, D. (2018). Macroeconomic conditions, inequality shocks and the politics of redistribution, 1990-2013. *Journal of European Public Policy, 25*(1), 31-58.

Popper, K. (2002 [1963]). *Conjectures and refutations. The growth of scientific knowledge.* Routledge.

Porter, R. (1997). *Medicine: A history of healing.* Barnes & Noble Books.

Rehm, P. (2011). Social policy by popular demand. *World Politics, 63*(2), 271-299.

Rehm, P. (2016). *Risk inequality and welfare states.* Cambridge and New York: Cambridge University Press.

Rimlinger, G. V. (1971). *Welfare policy and industrialization in Europe, America and Russia.* New York: Wiley.

Robertson, D. B. (1976). *A theory of party competition.* John Wiley & Sons.

Rueda, D. (2007). *Social democracy inside out: Partisanship and labor market policy in advanced industrialized democracies.* Oxford University Press.

Sell, A., Bryant, G. A., Cosmides, L., Tooby, J., Sznycer, D., Von Rueden, C., & Gurven, M. (2010). Adaptations in humans for assessing physical strength from the voice. *Proceedings of the Royal Society of London B: Biological Sciences, 277*(1699), 3509-3518.

Sell, A., Cosmides, L., Tooby, J., Sznycer, D., von Rueden, C., & Gurven, M. (2009a). Human adaptations for the visual assessment of strength and fighting ability from the body and face. *Proceedings of the Royal Society of London B: Biological Sciences, 276*(1656), 575-584.

Sell, A., Tooby, J., & Cosmides, L. (2009b). Formidability and the logic of human anger. *Proceedings of the National Academy of Sciences, 106*(35), 15073-15078.

Sigelman, L., & Buell, E. H. (2004). Avoidance or engagement? Issue convergence in US presidential campaigns, 1960-2000. *American Journal of Political Science, 48*(4), 650-661.

Simon, H. (1997 [1945]). *Administrative behavior.* Simon and Schuster.

Stanovich, K. (2011). *Rationality and the reflective mind.* Oxford University Press.

Steinmo, S., & Watts, J. (1995). It's the institutions, stupid! Why comprehensive national health insurance always fails in America. *Journal of Health Politics, Policy and Law, 20*(2), 329-372.

Stephens, J. D. (1979), *The transition from socialism to capitalism.* Urbana, Ill.: University of Illinois Press.

Stone, D. (2011). *Policy paradox. The art of political decision making.* WW Norton.

Streeck, W., & Thelen, K. (2005), Introduction: Institutional Change in Advanced Political Economies. In W. Streeck & K. Thelen (eds.), *Beyond continuity. Institutional change in advanced political economies* (pp. 1-39). Oxford: Oxford University Press.

Stubager, R. (2008). Education effects on authoritarian–libertarian values: A question of socialization. *The British Journal of Sociology, 59*(2), 327-350.

Sugiyama, L. S. (2004). Illness, injury, and disability among Shiwiar forager-horticulturalists: Implications of health-risk buffering for the evolution of human life history. *American Journal of Physical Anthropology, 123*(4), 371-389.

Sugiyama, L. S., & Chacon, R. (2000). Effects of illness and injury on foraging among the Yora and Shiwiar: Pathology risk as adaptive problem. In L. Cronk, N. Chagnon, & W. Irons (eds.), *Human behavior and adaptation: An anthropological perspective* (pp. 371-395). New York: Aldine De Gruyter.

Swenson, P. (2002). *Capitalists against markets: The making of labor markets and welfare states in the United States and Sweden.* Oxford University Press.

Swenson, P. (2017). *Business power and the welfare state: Comment on Walter Korpi and his Power resources and employer-centered approaches.* Working paper.

Thane, P. (2000). *Old age in English history: Past experiences, present issues.* Oxford University Press.

Thelen, K. (2014). *Varieties of liberalization and the new politics of social solidarity.* Cambridge University Press.

Thomson, R., Royed, T., Naurin, E., Artés, J., Costello, R., Ennser-Jedenastik, L., et al. (2017). The fulfillment of parties' election pledges: A comparative study on the impact of power sharing. *American Journal of Political Science, 61*(3), 527-542.

Tooby, J., & Cosmides, L. (1992). The psychological foundations of culture. In J. Barkow, L. Cosmides, & J. Tooby (eds.), *The adapted mind: Evolutionary psychology and the generation of culture.* Oxford University Press.

Tsebelis, G. (2002). *Veto players: How political institutions work.* Princeton University Press.

van Kersbergen, K. (1995), *Social capitalism: A study of Christian democracy and the welfare state.* London and New York: Routledge.

van Kersbergen, K., & Manow, P. (2009). *Religion, Class Coalitions, and Welfare States.* Cambridge: Cambridge University Press.

van Oorschot, W. (2000). Who should get what and why? On deservingness criteria and the conditionality of solidarity among the public. *Policy and Politics, 28*(1), 33-48.

van Oorschot, W. (2006). Making the difference in social Europe: Deservingness perceptions among citizens of European welfare states. *Journal of European Social Policy, 16*(1), 23-42.

Visser, P. S., & Mirabile, R. R. (2004). Attitudes in the social context: The impact of social network composition on individual-level attitude strength. *Journal of Personality and Social Psychology, 87*(6), 779.

Wilensky, H. L. (1975), *The welfare state and equality: Structural and ideological roots of public expenditures.* Berkeley: University of California Press.

Wilensky, H. L., & Lebeaux, C. N. (1958). *Industrial society and social welfare: The impact of industrialization on the supply and organization of social welfare services in the united states.* New York: Russell Sage Foundation.

Wlezien, C. (1995). The public as thermostat: Dynamics of preferences for spending. *American Journal of Political Science, 39*(4), 981-1000.

World Health Organization (2015). *World report on ageing and health 2015.* World Health Organization.

Wren, A., & Rehm, P. (2014). The end of the consensus? Labour market developments and the politics of retrenchment. *Socio-Economic Review, 12*(2), 409-435.

Zohlnhöfer, R., Wolf, F., & Wenzelburger, G. (2013). Political parties and pension generosity in times of permanent austerity. *World Political Science, 9*(1), 291-318.